The New Oxford Picture Dictionary

Listening and Speaking Activity Book

The New Oxford Picture Dictionary

Listening and Speaking Activity Book

Jayme Adelson-Goldstein, Rheta Goldman,
Norma Shapiro, and Renée Weiss

Oxford University Press

Oxford University Press
200 Madison Avenue
New York, NY 10016 USA

Walton Street
Oxford OX2 6DP England

OXFORD is a trademark of Oxford University Press.

Library of Congress Cataloging-in-Publication Data

The New Oxford picture dictionary listening and
    speaking activity book/Jayme Adelson-Goldstein . . .
    [et al.].
        p.   cm.
    ISBN 0-19-434365-0
        1. English language—Textbooks for foreign speakers.
        2. English language—Spoken English—Problems,
    exercises, etc.   3. Listening—Problems,
    exercises, etc.   I. Adelson-Goldstein, Jayme.
    II. Title: Listening and speaking activity book.
    PE1128.N393   1992
    428.3′4—dc20   92-8821
                                                         CIP

Editorial Manager: Susan Lanzano
Developmental Editor: Helen Munch
Senior Designer: Mark Kellogg
Art Buyer/Picture Researcher: Karen Polyak
Production Manager: Abram Hall

Printing (last digit):   10 9 8 7 6 5 4 3 2 1

Printed in the United States of America.

Cover illustration by Laura Maestro.

Interior illustrations by David Cain, Jennifer Dubnau,
Patrick Girouard, Ethel Gold, Maj-Britt Hagsted, Frank
Magadan, Tom Sperling, and Stephan Van Litsenborg.

Contents

Acknowledgments

The authors gratefully acknowledge the love, patience, and support of their families: Norma's Neil, Eli, and Alex; Renée's Malcolm and Sophie Rose; Jayme's Gary and Emily Rose; and Rheta's Alan. "What, another meeting?"

Of course, we would never have begun or completed this book without the professionalism, expertise, and gourmet tastes of our editors, Susan Lanzano, Helen Munch, and Pat O'Neill. "What, another comma?" We would also like to acknowledge the teachers, students, and staff of Van Nuys Community Adult School and North Hollywood Learning Center, as well as our colleagues in the Los Angeles Unified School District for their encouragement. "What, another book?"

And finally, special thanks to Doctors Ronald Leuchter, Peter Rosen, and Edward Sigall for keeping our group together.

Introduction

The *New Oxford Picture Dictionary Listening and Speaking Activity Book* is a teacher-friendly collection of beginning-level ESL communicative activities based on topics and vocabulary in *The New Oxford Picture Dictionary*. This classroom-tested collection contains activities incorporating a variety of ESL techniques, such as focused listening, cooperative learning, information gap, role play, and language experience approach, as well as drills and games.

ORGANIZATION

The *Listening and Speaking Activity Book* is divided into 12 units of eight activities each (three to four listening activities followed by four to five speaking activities). A unit opener page introduces each unit, briefly describing the unit's activities. A page of Answer Cards and seven Picture Card pages follow the final unit.

Units

The first 11 units are organized around specific topics and pages found in the mono-lingual English edition of *The New Oxford Picture Dictionary,* available in hardcover and paper-back. These units include the listening and speaking activities plus Teacher's Notes and reproducible activity sheets.

While the units follow the sequence of the Dictionary pages, they can be used in any order. In addition, since different topics may share the same target vocabulary, some activities reference the same Dictionary page(s).

The final unit, *All-Around Activities,* can be used with any of the Dictionary pages.

Activities

The eight listening and speaking activities within each unit center around a life-skill area. For example, *Talking About Jobs,* refers to the Occupations pages of the Dictionary and includes activities requiring students to practice listening for job salary and schedule information, following on-the-job directions, and interviewing for a job.

The activities are of different types (listen and point, information gap, role play, and so on) and are identified by title and type on the unit opener pages and in the Teacher's Notes for each activity.

The *All-Around Activities* include a number of updated old favorites, such as chain drills, brainstorms, and quiz games, which can be used with any Dictionary topic or page. Following the Teacher's Notes for each *All-Around Activity* is a chart suggesting how to adapt the activity for use with any of the topics presented in the preceding 11 units.

Teacher's Notes

The Teacher's Notes for each of the 96 activities provide helpful mini-lesson plans for beginning level students, as well as "Variation" ideas for multi-level classes.

Activity type, time, student grouping, materials, and focus are highlighted at the top of each Teacher's Notes page, followed by a "Before class" statement informing teachers of any necessary preparation.

The lesson plan, with numbered steps, is divided into the following stages:
Preview: Students review the Dictionary topic and target vocabulary.
Presentation: The teacher models the activity and reviews the directions.
Practice: Students perform the activity or complete a task.
Follow-up: Students apply or extend what they've learned.
Variation(s): Teachers modify an activity and/or make it easier or more challenging.

Tapescripts and Answers

Tapescripts for the focused listening activities appear at the end of the Teacher's Notes for a particular activity. Where appropriate, answers are also provided either in the tapescript or separately.

Student Activity Sheets

Following the Teacher's Notes for each unit are four pages of reproducible student activity sheets. Although some activities require only the use of the Dictionary and/or paper and pencil, most require a matching student activity sheet. The activity sheets in each unit feature one or two activities per sheet. The activity title (and corresponding Teacher's Notes page) is clearly identified, as are cut lines when more than one activity appears on a sheet.

ACTIVITY TYPES

Several activity types are used repeatedly throughout *The New Oxford Picture Dictionary Listening and Speaking Activity Book.* The activity types can be categorized as follows:

Listening Activities	Speaking Activities
Silent Drill	Interview
Listen and Point	Class Search/Mixer/Drill
Listen and Check	Game
Listen and Circle	Information Gap
Listening Grid	TPR Pair/Group
Listen and Sequence	Cooperative Learning/ Brainstorm
Listen and Draw	Role Play
Listen and Number	Language Experience

The activity types are described below with suggestions (■) on how to implement each activity.

Listening Activities

There are two types of listening activities in the book: vocabulary comprehension checks and focused listening activities. The focused listening activities use cassette recordings of real-life listening situations.

Silent Drill is a listening activity that offers teachers a way to evaluate student comprehension of the vocabulary on a specific Dictionary page. Students respond independently to the teacher's questions by holding up a *Yes/No/Not Sure* card. The teacher sees at a glance how many of the students understand the vocabulary.

■ Have students keep a set of the *Yes/No/Not Sure* answer cards at their desks, ready for use with any Dictionary page.

Focused listening activities teach active listening that students can apply to real-life situations. Students listen to recorded monologues and focus on specific information embedded within the listening passage. While students are listening, they are asked to perform simple tasks, such as pointing to or circling the correct information. These tasks allow students at the earliest stages of language learning to demonstrate the accuracy of their listening. Although the written tasks are simple, the listening activities themselves are quite challenging.

Listen and Point: Students look at a page in the Dictionary, listen to a monologue, and point to the items or people being described.

Listen and Check and *Listening Grid:* Students listen to a series of statements and make checks in the correct categories on their activity sheets.

Listen and Circle: Students listen for cues in a series of statements in order to circle the correct word on their activity sheets.

Listen and Sequence: Students listen to a series of statements or a story and identify the sequence of pictures or actions on their activity sheets.

Listen and Draw: Students listen to a series of commands instructing them where to draw or write on their activity sheets.

Listen and Number: Students listen to a monologue and match vocabulary with the pictures in their Dictionaries.

■ Be sure to preview the target vocabulary in the tapescripts prior to beginning the activity in class. Focused listening activities teach students to listen for previously acquired vocabulary. They do not teach the vocabulary itself.

■ Reassure students that they will hear the listening passage up to five times, and encourage students to listen beyond the interference of unfamiliar words.

■ Use the accompanying listening cassette so that you can pause between exercise items, repeat a single item, and review the entire listening passage without changing the intonation, stress, or speed of the language. The cassette recording will also bring other voices into the classroom, giving you the freedom to facilitate and monitor student progress.

Speaking Activities

All of the speaking activities are task-based. Students practice speaking in order to exchange information or complete a specific project. After students understand the goal of the activity, they are given a time limit and assisted during the practice by their peers and teacher.

Interview: Students share personal preferences and information as they practice asking and answering *yes/no* and *Wh*-questions. In non-threatening small groups, students find out about their classmates and discover what they have in common.

■ Group students heterogeneously by language, gender, age, or ability so that the groups will be more interactive.

Class Search, Mixer, and *Drill* activities give students communicative practice in a topic area, using a specific set of structures. After the teacher has modeled the language to be used, students practice with one another.

Class Search: Students receive an activity sheet with "Find someone who can . . ." statements and transform the statements into *yes/no* questions. Students then walk around the classroom asking the *yes/no* questions in order to complete the search.

Mixer: Students walk around the room using cue slips to help them generate questions and answers appropriate to specific situations, such as a family party or a hospital waiting room. Several different drill activities are used throughout the book.

Chain Drill: Students take turns repeating a sentence modeled by the teacher, adding a new vocabulary item each time.

Interactive Drill and *Circle Drill:* Students use an activity sheet, props, or cue slips to help them generate questions that follow a specific structural pattern. Students ask and answer the questions, substituting different vocabulary items.

Games provide enjoyable interactive practice of specific topic area language. Many games use the Picture Cards as cues or specific Dictionary pages. Once familiar with a game's particular format, students can play the game with any topic area, each time reinforcing different vocabulary. Several different game types are introduced in the book.

Board Game: Students follow directions to move around a game board answering questions, recalling specific vocabulary, and spelling words correctly.

Quiz Game: Students, in teams, write questions about a specific Dictionary page in order to test the opposing team's recall of information on that page. Students set the level of difficulty for the activity by creating the questions for the game.

Matching and *TPR Game:* Students use Picture Cards, word cards, and grids in games similar to *Concentration* and *Battleship.* Students play in pairs at their own speed.

■ Use board games to evaluate student progress in a topic area.

■ Assign more able students as "referees" to circulate and monitor group progress.

Information Gaps offer students an opportunity to practice questions and answers within a specific framework while providing a degree of unpredictability. Paired students use similar activity sheets with different information missing from each sheet. Partners ask for and provide the missing information, using the questions on the activity sheets and their own resources. Each activity sheet includes a different clarification strategy to help students complete their task, such as "How much?" or "Where?"

■ Be aware that students unsure of the language required often look at their partner's paper or use their first language. To alleviate this problem, pair weaker students with stronger ones and, wherever possible, pair students with different native languages.

TPR Pair and *TPR Group* activities progress from teacher commanding students to students commanding teacher, to students commanding students. In a TPR pair activity, students work together in leader/follower roles, giving and carrying out a series of commands. In a TPR group activity, students work together to write a series of commands. Group leaders then circulate, giving the commands to other groups. Students with different learning styles benefit from TPR activities. Kinesthetic learners relate to drawing, visual learners to visual cues, and auditory learners to oral directions.

■ Make sure students receive a lot of teacher modeling and whole class practice with the language, and are comfortable with the structure of the commands.

Cooperative Learning activities offer more challenging situations and motivate students to participate equally, learn from one another, and work toward a common goal. Students work together and depend upon one another, but they are also individually accountable for their task in an activity. Cooperative activities improve listening skills, increase problem-solving abilities, and enhance critical thinking skills. Different examples of cooperative learning activities used in this book follow.

Cooperative Sequencing, Stories, Jigsaws, and *Questions:* Students work together to sequence events, tell a story, complete a group task using shared resources (picture or word cues), or answer questions about a specific Dictionary page.

Brainstorm: Students generate lists of vocabulary and ideas in small cooperative groups by circulating a single piece of paper. Group members jot down their contributions and pass around the paper as many times as possible.

■ Be sure students are clear from the start about the task and have developed group rapport and respect by learning one another's names, backgrounds, and a few other details. Use one of the Interview activities, such as *Food Survey* (p. 20) to break the ice.

■ Be patient with students. Your efforts will pay off. (See *Classroom Management Tips,* below, for more suggestions.)

Role Plays allow students to apply previously learned language in a variety of real-life situations, such as ordering food, responding to a doctor's commands, or answering job interview questions. Students also practice different language functions and registers, such as asking for clarification, interrupting, hesitating, and disagreeing. For each role play, the teacher—acting as manager, observer, and/or participant during the role play—provides a sequence of events and elicits appropriate language for each step of

the sequence. Students then review the language and see a demonstration role play *before* participating in it.

■ Use simple props to set the scene and make the role play more realistic.

■ Encourage students to stretch their language abilities.

■ Try videotaping the role play, then use the tape for a follow-up class discussion.

Language Experience activities allow students to read what they can already say. Students work on a class project, such as designing a city, making fruit salad, or making a quilt. When finished, students dictate the story of their project to the teacher or to another student. The story is written on the board exactly as dictated, with students given opportunities to edit along the way. Students then *read* the story they already know and have produced. The goal of language experience activities is to get students communicating about a common class experience, using the skills of listening, speaking, reading, and writing.

■ For best results, assemble all materials in advance.

■ To facilitate the Practice stage of the activity, assign individual tasks, such as collecting materials or monitoring first language use. (See "Numbered Heads," p. xvi, for more information.)

■ Try not to overcorrect students' oral dictations. Blatant errors may be questioned, but additional editing is not required if students are content with their final version.

CLASSROOM MANAGEMENT TIPS

Assembling Materials

Be sure to check the "Before class" section of the Teacher's Notes for the required number of copies of the student activity sheet. Many of the activities are for pair or group work and do not require individual copies of the materials.

When an activity calls for picture or cue cards to be cut apart to create sets, have students do the cutting as a TPR activity. (Don't forget to include this preparation step in your lesson plan.)

Save the materials in small envelopes for future activities.

If you work with a paper cutter and find it tedious to clip together sets of materials, create a classroom assembly line and have students do the work for you. Do not, however, let students cut apart and/or clip together picture sequence sets or the goal of that particular activity will be lost!

Comprehension Checks

Checking for student understanding of activity content, procedure, or goal can be done non-verbally and/or by having students paraphrase your directions or answer some brief questions. While the *Yes/No/Not Sure* cards (p. 179) are designed for use with Silent Drill activities, they also provide an excellent way to check for comprehension in other activities. After making a class set of the cards, have students keep them available at their desks. Use the cards for quick individual assessments by asking *yes/no* questions about the target vocabulary, activity context or topic, or directions. The Silent Drill cards can also be used for comprehension checks between the Presentation and Practice stages of an activity. For example, after presenting a series of directions to the class, ask students *yes/no* questions, such as "Do you write your answers?" or "If you don't understand something, can you ask a friend?" to determine comprehension. This simple check will help prevent any major misunderstandings during the Practice stage.

First Language Interference and Copying

If students are using their first language excessively, you need to examine the reasons. Perhaps the activity is too difficult or students need more practice. Try modeling clarification questions, such as "How do you say that?"; "Could you repeat that?"; and "What does this mean?" to help students express their needs in English.

If your students are always looking at one another's papers, they are probably insecure with the task, not prepared, or feel they need a perfect paper. Reassure students that they will have a chance to correct their papers at the end of the activity. Use humor to demonstrate the be-

havior you don't want, by saying to your Japanese students, "No Spanish, please," and to your Spanish-speaking students, "No Japanese, please," or by pantomiming "peeking" at a student's paper. Realize that cheating may be a culture-bound behavior and that what you may interpret as "cheating" may in fact be one student's way of helping another.

Grouping Strategies

The act of grouping students in pairs or small groups is a communicative activity in itself. The way students are grouped facilitates their speaking practice by alleviating the problem of first language interference and non-participation.

The ideal groups have some degree of heterogeneity in terms of ethnicity, language, gender, age, or ability. Use a mixer to pair students, then combine pairs to produce heterogeneous groups. (A few adjustments may be necessary.) Or, cut magazine pictures into four or five separate pieces, randomly distribute them, and have students find the missing pieces of their picture.

To form pairs, distribute Picture Cards from the *All-Around Activities* unit to half the class, and word cards you've created to the other half. Then ask students to match pictures with words.

To create groups of mixed ability in classes with regularly attending students, you can make seating (name) cards ahead of time. As students enter the classroom, they look for their cards and know where to sit. Each time students are grouped, be sure they know one another's names and share a little information about themselves before the activity begins.

Monitoring

When monitoring an activity, try to assess how the activity is going and if it is meeting your students' needs. This is the time for students to be practicing. It's best not to interrupt students with numerous corrections; rather, make a mental note of problem areas for future instruction. You can monitor a listening activity by observing your students' progress. Stay close to the tape recorder while it is playing, but move around the room when you stop the tape, to check responses. During speaking activities, circulate among students to observe their progress and to answer any questions.

"Numbered Heads" (Role and Task Assignments)

Assigning roles or tasks encourages students to take responsibility for their group's progress and allows you to facilitate rather than run an activity. Before beginning an activity in small groups, have students assign themselves a number—one to four or five. Give each numbered student a different job, such as distributing/collecting the materials, time-keeping, recording responses, or monitoring first language use.

Overhead Projectors (OHPs)

Teachers fortunate enough to have an OHP in their classroom will find using transparencies very helpful. With transparencies, the entire class can focus on all or a portion of an activity sheet at the same time, while listening to your directions and explanations. You and any student volunteers can write directly on the transparency to model an example and to verify correct responses. An OHP is especially useful in the presentation of games, such as *Back and Forth Bingo* and *Twin Grids*.

You may also want to use the *Overhead Transparencies* available for *The New Oxford Picture Dictionary*. By selectively masking and/or pointing, you can focus on any part of a Dictionary page you wish. You may want to mask parts of an illustration, drawing attention to certain items or you may prefer to work with certain words only, masking the others. You may wish to cover the words and elicit vocabulary from the students or unmask the words one by one, drawing attention to each word as you do so. *The New Oxford Picture Dictionary* transparencies feature every page of the monolingual English edition of the Dictionary.

Props and Realia

The use of props and realia brings to life many classroom activities, especially role plays. Tell students a few days ahead that they will be having a garage sale or a health fair, or running a restaurant. The advance notice will help build excitement and remind students of any materials, props, or supplies they need to bring from home. (Two of the language experience activities, for example, *Fruit Salad for 30* and *A Friend-ship Quilt*, ask students to bring in supplies.) Keep extra supplies on hand in case students are absent or forget.

Quiet Signals

A quiet signal is the best way to capture students' attention rapidly during pair, group, or whole class speaking activities. Teachers use a variety of signals for quiet: a raised hand, a bell, lights flicked on and off. Whatever signal you choose, be sure to vary it every few weeks so that it retains its punch.

Getting Together
Teacher's Notes and Activity Sheets

Who Are They?

Focus: Identifying kinship terms.

Materials: Answer Cards and Don't Look Mask, p. 179; **People and Relationships, Dictionary, p. 2.**

Before class, duplicate and cut apart a class set of the Answer Cards and Don't Look Mask. Look over the silent drill questions and the target vocabulary (step 4 below).

Preview

1. Hold up a set of answer cards and tell students that they will be listening to and answering a series of questions by raising the correct answer card.
2. Direct students to open their dictionaries to page 2. Ask students to identify the people in the pictures (husband, wife, son, daughter). Talk about the relationships between them.

Presentation

3. Distribute the answer cards and the masks. Have students cover the vocabulary at the bottom of the page and listen to your questions about the pictures. Ask the first question: "Look at #1. Is this a *woman?*" Tell students to raise the Yes card if the answer is yes, the No card if it is no, and the Not Sure card when there's not enough information to answer yes or no. Get class consensus on the first answer before continuing.

Practice (with Answers)

4. Ask the following questions:
   Look at #1. Is this a *woman?* (Yes)
   Look at #2. Is this a *baby?* (No)
   Look at #3 and #4. Are they *brother* and *sister?* (No)
   Look at #5. Is this a *wife?* (No)
   Look at #6. Are they *parents?* (Yes)
   Look at #7. Are they *children?* (Yes)
   Look at #9. Is this a *mother?* (No)
   Look at #10. Are they the *parents* of the young woman in the photo? (Not sure)
   Look at #11. Is this a *wife?* (No)
   Look at #12. Is this a *husband?* (No)

Follow-up

5. Have students talk about the photos on page 2 and decide the order in which they might have been taken.

Mary Smith's Family Tree

Focus: Identifying family relationships.

Materials: Don't Look Mask, p. 179; listening cassette; **The Family, Dictionary, p. 3.**

Before class, duplicate a class set of the Don't Look Mask. Look over the target vocabulary in the tapescript below.

Preview

1. Tell students that they will be listening to Mary Smith talk about her family.·
2. Direct students to open their dictionaries to page 3. Tell them to look for the woman in the blue square, and identify her as Mary Smith. See if students can find Sally and Tim and tell you Mary's husband's name.
3. Draw a small family tree (three or four family members) on the board to illustrate the concept of relatives. Tell students, "This is Mary Smith. Sally and Tim are her children. Mary is their mother."

Presentation

4. Distribute the masks and have students cover the vocabulary at the bottom of the page. Tell students to listen to the tape and to point to the correct pictures in their dictionaries. Assure students that they will have several opportunities to hear the listening passage.
5. Play the tape through "I'm so glad we're married." Stop the tape and check to be sure that students are pointing to picture #12. Replay this section of the tape until all students are pointing to picture #12.

Practice

6. Play the tape, stopping when necessary. Replay the tape two to five times.

Follow-up

7. Check for comprehension of the target vocabulary by pointing to #12 and asking, "Who is he?" Students can respond in a number of different ways, including "That's Bob Smith. He's Mary's husband." "He's Tim's father." "He's Peg's uncle."

Variation

To make this activity more challenging, have students use Mary's family tree as the basis for drawing up their own family trees. Tell students to write some sentences describing their family relationships.

Tapescript (with Answers)

Listen to Mary Smith talk about her family. Point to the pictures of her relatives.

Hi, I'm Mary Smith. I'd like to introduce you to some of the people in my family. My *husband (12)*, Bob Smith, is on the right. Bob's a terrific *husband (12)*. I'm so glad we're married.* We have two lovely children. Our *son (16)*, Tim, is nine and our *daughter (15)*, Sally, is seven. They're great kids but sometimes. . .well, you know.* I have a *sister (10)*, Jane, and she's married to a sweet guy, Tom Carter. He's my favorite *brother-in-law (11)*.* My *niece (14)*, Peg, is their daughter. People always say Peg and I look a lot alike.* Do you see my *brother (9)*, Jack? Jack's a professional singer and three years ago he married Betty, a piano player.* My *sister-in-law (8)* and Jack have the cutest little boy, my *nephew (13)*, Jimmy. He's a nice child—not like my Tim—but still a nice boy.* Can you find my *father (5)*, Tom? He loves to cook, so when he retired this year he moved into the kitchen. My mom, Elizabeth, is a great lady, but having Dad in the kitchen was too much for her. Now *mother (4)* has a job and everybody's happy.* Here's the most confusing part about my family. I have an *Aunt (6)* Helen. She's my father's sister. My *Uncle (3)* Peter is married to Ellen, not Helen, and they are my *cousin (7)* Joan's parents.* Joan and I are good friends. We love to get together. In fact, we're going to get together this weekend, when my *grandmother (1)*, Virginia, and *grandfather (2)*, Joseph, celebrate their 60th wedding anniversary.* Everyone in my family is coming to our house. Oh my goodness, everyone in my family is coming here!! Uh, excuse me, I have to start cooking and cleaning now!

Who's Coming to Dinner?

Focus: Identifying family members by gender.

Materials: Activity sheet, p. 11; listening cassette; **The Family, Dictionary, p. 3.**

Before class, duplicate a class set of the activity sheet. Look over the target vocabulary in the tapescript below.

Preview

1. Tell students that they will be listening to Jane Carter talk about who's coming to her family dinner party.
2. Direct students to open their dictionaries to page 3 and study the vocabulary and family tree for 60 seconds. Have students close their dictionaries and tell you the names of as many family members as they can remember and their relationship to Jane Carter (Mary/sister). List students' responses on the board, then ask students to identify which of the family members are male and which are female.

Presentation

3. Copy one set of the male and female stick figures and the example from the activity sheet onto the board. Explain the task to the students, and assure them that they will have several opportunities to hear the listening passage.
4. Have students listen to the tape through "... my *grandmother's* birthday," and review the example on the board.
5. Distribute the activity sheets and review the directions.

Practice

6. Play the tape, stopping when necessary.
7. Take a survey of the number of checks made under each stick figure in A. Get class consensus on the accuracy of the numbers. If class response is inaccurate, have students repeat the activity using the second set of figures (B). If necessary, replay the tape a third time, using the third set of figures (C).
8. Invite a volunteer to do the activity on the board as you play the tape one last time.

Follow-up

9. Ask students to list all the "titles" they hold in their own families, such as mother, sister, wife, aunt, niece, and daughter, for females. Have students use People and Relationships, and The Family (pages 2 and 3 in their dictionaries) for reference. Then have students form small groups to compare lists.

Tapescript (with Answers)

Listen to Jane Carter talk about her family. Make a check in the correct box.

We moved into this apartment last week and I'm having a family dinner party tonight. You see, it's my *grandmother's* birthday.* No one in my family has seen this new apartment except my *sister*, Mary. She helped me find it.* Mary's coming tonight, of course, with my *brother-in-law*, Bob.* Bob and Mary are coming early to help me. They're bringing my *niece*, Sally. She's seven years old and she likes to help, too.* I invited my favorite *aunt*, Helen. We don't see her very often because she doesn't drive.* Tonight she's coming with my *brother*, Jack. Jack lives on the other side of the city, near her house.* I asked my *husband*, Tom, to stop on his way home from work and pick up my *mother* at her office. Her office isn't far from Tom's. I'm very busy cooking and getting ready. I want everything to be perfect tonight.

(**Answers:** Females—5 checks; Males—3 checks.)

The Family Draw

Focus: Identifying family relationships.

Materials: Activity sheet, p. 12; listening cassette; **People and Relationships, Dictionary, p. 2.**

Before class, duplicate a class set of the activity sheet. Look over the target vocabulary in the tapescript below.

Follow-up

7. Draw sets of four circles on the board, similar to those on the activity sheet. Divide the class into teams and have students from each team come to the board. Direct the students to draw features on the family members and to connect them according to your directions. Team members can take turns coming to the board.

Preview

1. Tell students that they will be listening to sentences about families and drawing lines to connect the members of each family.
2. Direct students to open their dictionaries to page 2 and look over the photographs. Help students identify the family relationships by asking yes/no questions, such as "Look at #1—Is she a woman?"; "Is she a husband?"

Presentation

3. Distribute the activity sheets and review the directions. Assure students that they will have several opportunities to hear the listening passage.
4. Play the tape through number 1 ". . . from the man to the woman." Stop the tape and review the example by having students tell you how the lines connect the family members.

Practice

5. Play the tape, stopping after each item. When necessary, replay each item two to five times.
6. Have students, in pairs, compare their completed activity sheets to see if their family drawings match.

Tapescript (with Answers)

Listen to each sentence. Look at the pictures. Draw a line to connect the people in each family.
1. Draw a line from the *girl* to the *boy,* from the *boy* to the *man,* from the *man* to the *woman.*
2. Draw a line from the *husband* to the *wife,* from the *wife* to the *son,* from the *son* to the *daughter.*
3. Draw a line from the *son* to his *mother,* from his *mother* to his *sister,* from his *sister* to his *father.*
4. Draw a line from the *daughter* to her *father,* from her *father* to her *brother,* from her *brother* to her *mother.*
5. Draw a line from the *son* to his *mother,* from his *mother* to her *husband,* from her *husband* to his *daughter,* from his *daughter* to her *cousin.*
6. Draw a line from the *woman* to the *man,* from the *man* to the *boy,* from the *boy* to the *girl.*

Around the Table

Focus: Asking for and giving information on seating arrangements.

Materials: Activity sheet, p. 13; manila folders (one per pair); 14 4" x 6" index cards; **The Family, Dictionary, p. 3.**

Before class, duplicate half a class set of the activity sheet. Cut apart the A and B sections of the sheets and keep them separate. Write the following names on the 14 index cards (one name per card): Virginia, Jack, Joseph, Betty, Peg, Tom, Elizabeth, Helen, Ellen, Peter, Joan, Bob, Sally, and Tim. Copy the conversation from the activity sheet onto the board.

Preview

1. Tell students that they will be working in pairs to find out the missing names on a seating chart.
2. Direct students to open their dictionaries to page 3. On the board, draw a table with six chairs. Ask students to list six members of Mary Smith's family on the board (Betty, Tom, Jack, Elizabeth, and so on). Write three of the family members' names on three chairs. Then have students tell you where the remaining three relatives will sit. Write the names on the remaining chairs.

Presentation

3. Use the conversation on the board to model the language and clarification strategy you want students to use in the activity. Have the class practice the conversation, substituting different family members' names.
4. Pair students and assign each one an A or a B role. Explain to students that they will each have a seating chart with different names missing. Point out that the missing names are on their partner's seating chart. Tell students that they will take turns asking for and giving the missing names in order to complete their charts.

5. Distribute a manila folder to each pair, to be propped up between the students as a screen. Distribute the A and B activity sheets to the appropriate partners. Review the directions and instruct students to look only at their own papers and not at their partner's.
6. Tell students to look at the example on their seating charts and to tell you who is sitting across from Bob. Check comprehension by asking A students, "Who's sitting across from Helen?" Ask B students, "Who is sitting across from Virginia?"
7. Have one pair demonstrate the activity by asking for and giving names from their seating charts. Remind students to look only at their own charts.

Practice

8. Have students, in pairs, ask and answer questions about the missing people on their seating charts. Once they complete the task, partners can compare charts to be sure they are the same.

Follow-up

9. Have students open their dictionaries to page 3 and identify Mary's relationship to each person at the table. Ask students to name the people who are not at the party.
10. Have students close their dictionaries and turn their seating charts face down. Distribute the 14 index cards to 14 volunteers. Ask the volunteers to seat themselves (or stand) according to the completed seating chart. Have the rest of the class evaluate and assist the students in positioning themselves correctly.

Family Survey

> **Focus:** Discussing family.
>
> **Materials:** Activity sheet, p. 11;
> **People and Relationships,**
> **Dictionary, p. 2.**
>
> ───────────────────────
>
> *Before class, duplicate a class set of
> the activity sheet.*

Preview

1. Tell students that they will be interviewing their classmates and talking about their families.
2. Direct students to open their dictionaries to page 2. Ask students to name the family members in each photograph. Be sure to include the relationships given on the activity sheet (children, brother, sister). Discuss marital status: single, married, divorced, widowed.

Presentation

3. Copy the grid from the activity sheet onto the board. Model the questions from the grid: "What's your marital status?"; "How many children do you have?"; and so on. Using the grid on the board, write your name in the first column and have the class ask you the first question. Answer the question about yourself and write your answer in the grid box. Explain that only short answers are written in the boxes below the questions.
4. Ask a volunteer to come to the board. Write the student's name under your name on the grid. Have different students ask the volunteer one question each from the grid. Write the answers on the grid.

Practice

5. Divide the class into groups of four and distribute an activity sheet to each student.
6. Have students take turns asking the questions of the person on their left, while the other group members listen and write the answers on their grids. When students have completed their grids, they can use the information to discuss the questions below the grid.
7. Set a 20-minute time limit for students to complete the task. Circulate and monitor student practice.

Follow-up

8. Use the grid on the board to elicit responses from each group. Number the groups and write the group numbers in the first column. Ask the survey questions and write the groups' responses on the board. Continue asking the groups all the questions, writing the single majority response wherever possible. If each group member has a different answer, write "varies."
9. When you've finished interviewing all the groups, have students use your completed survey to comment on patterns in the class.

Variations

To make this activity easier, conduct a teacher-directed survey with the whole class.

To make this activity more challenging, have groups generate three additional items to include in their survey.

Louise Brown's Photo Album

Focus: Identifying and describing family relationships.

Materials: Don't Look Mask, p. 179; listening cassette; a few of your own family photos; **People and Relationships, Dictionary, p. 2.**

Before class, duplicate a class set of the Don't Look Mask. Look over the tapescript below.

Preview

1. Tell students that they will be listening to Louise Brown talk about her family and creating original stories based on the photographs.
2. Direct students to open their dictionaries to page 2. Have students identify Louise Brown by pointing as you describe her picture (#1). Tell students that all the pictures on this page are from Louise's family photo album.
3. Show a photo of your own family. Point to people as you identify their relationships and describe something about each person, such as "This is a picture of my cousin, Susan. She's standing next to me. She's my favorite cousin."

Presentation

4. Distribute the masks and have students cover the vocabulary at the bottom of the page. Tell students to listen to the tape and to point to the correct pictures in their dictionaries. Assure students that they will have several opportunities to hear the listening passage.
5. Have students listen to the tape through ". . . Louise Brown, as a young woman." Stop the tape and check to be sure that students are pointing to picture #1. Replay this section of the tape until all students are pointing to picture #1.

Practice

6. Play the tape, stopping when necessary. Replay the tape two to five times.
7. Divide the class into groups of six. Tell the class that each group will work together to create an original story about the pictures on Dictionary page 2. Assign each group a role as one member of Louise Brown's family: Bob, Alex, Sara, Peter, Michael, or Ana.
8. Set a 15-minute time limit for students to complete the task. Circulate and monitor student practice.

Follow-up

9. Have each group choose one volunteer to share the newly created family story with the whole class. Introduce students according to their chosen roles—"Bob Brown will now tell us about his photo album."

Tapescript

Listen to the story about Louise Brown. Point to the people Louise is talking about.

Oh, hello there. Do you want to see some pictures from my family album? Look at photograph #1. That's a picture of me, Louise Brown, as a young woman. I wasn't bad-looking.* On the right is a snapshot of Bob. Don't you think he's a handsome young man?* Oh, here's a wedding photo that shows our first day together as husband and wife. Today is our 50th anniversary, and we're still very happy together.* Do you see photo #5? Bob is holding our baby, Sara, in his arms.* In this same picture, Bob and I are standing in front of our new home. We were so proud the day we took that picture.* Take a look at picture #7. You see our two children, Alex the boy, and, of course, that's our little girl, Sara. Both our kids are grown now and have their own families.* Here's a recent photo with all of us together. Bob and I are very happy grandparents. I'm on the right, standing behind my wonderful grandson Michael. He loves sports.* Do you see Sara? She's standing between Bob and her husband Peter. Everyone says she looks like me when I was young.* And there's little Ana, our beautiful granddaughter. She's hiding next to Peter. . .I guess she's a little shy.

Arthur, This Is Bertha

Preview

1. Tell students that they are going to be members of Arthur and Bertha Green's family, meeting at the Green's wedding reception.
2. Direct students to open their dictionaries to page 2. Ask students to find the picture of the couple getting married (#3 and #4). Identify the couple as Arthur and Bertha Green. Have students imagine and talk about the couple's wedding reception.

Presentation

3. Copy the following conversation onto the board: Student 1: "Hello, I'm _____. I'm Arthur's cousin." Student 2: "Nice to meet you, _____. I'm _____. I'm Bertha's friend." Model the conversation for the class, then have the class practice, substituting different names.
4. Invite four volunteers to the front of the room and give each one an 8-1/2" x 11" cue slip. Have the volunteers look at their cues and introduce themselves to the class.

5. Demonstrate a third party introduction using the same four volunteers. "This is Carla, Bertha's sister." "This is José, Arthur's father." Then have the volunteers go through the "mixer" introducing themselves to one another.

Practice

6. Pair students and identify one partner as a member of Arthur's family (A), and the other as a member of Bertha's family (B).
7. Distribute the A cue slips to the A partners and the B cue slips to the B partners, making sure that they are gender appropriate. (If you have uneven numbers of men and women, use the cousin or friend cue slips.)
8. Have students introduce themselves to their partners. Tell students that they have 10 minutes to circulate, in pairs, and to meet the rest of the people at the "reception."

Follow-up

9. After the mixer, have partners write down the names of all the relatives (and friends) they met.

Variation

To make this activity more challenging, add a sentence to each cue slip on the activity sheet, directing students to find one particular person in the mixer (for example, "You are Bertha's uncle. You are looking for Arthur's father."). Have students "mix" to find the person named on their cue slips.

Your Notes

Who's Coming to Dinner? (See Teacher's Notes, page 4.)

- Listen to Jane Carter talk about her family.
- Make a check (√) in the correct box.

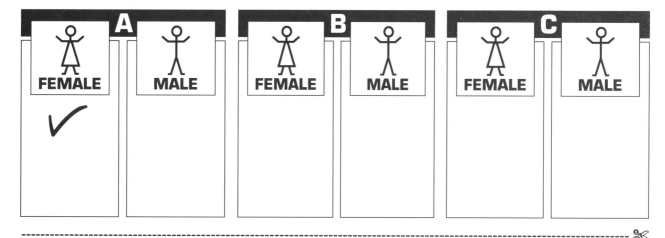

A		B		C	
FEMALE	MALE	FEMALE	MALE	FEMALE	MALE
√					

-- ✂

Family Survey (See Teacher's Notes, page 7.)

- Take turns asking and answering the questions about your family.
- Record the answers on the grid.

NAME	What's your marital status?	How many children do you have?	How many brothers do you have?	How many sisters do you have?	How many people are in your family?

- After you complete the grid, discuss these questions with your group:
  Who has the largest family?
  Do people in your group have more brothers or sisters?
  How many people in your group are married?

The Family Draw (See Teacher's Notes, page 5.)

- Listen to each sentence.
- Look at the pictures.
- Draw a line to connect the people in each family.

Around the Table (See Teacher's Notes, page 6.)

- Look at the seating chart below.
- Take turns asking your partner for the missing people's names.
- Write in the missing names.
- Use this conversation as a model:
    Who is sitting across from Bob?
    Jack.
    Can you spell that name for me?
    J-A-C-K, Jack.

A

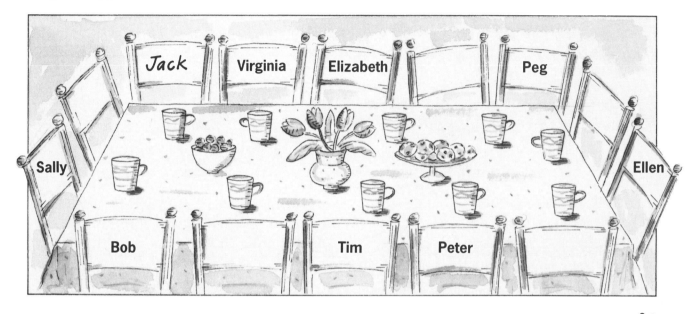

--- ✂

- Look at the seating chart below.
- Take turns asking your partner for the missing people's names.
- Write in the missing names.
- Use this conversation as a model:
    Who is sitting across from Bob?
    Jack.
    Can you spell that name for me?
    J-A-C-K, Jack.

B

Arthur, This Is Bertha (See Teacher's Notes, page 9.)

A Cue slips

Arthur's father
Arthur's mother
Arthur's sister
Arthur's brother
Arthur's aunt
Arthur's uncle
Arthur's brother-in-law
Arthur's sister-in-law
Arthur's niece
Arthur's nephew
Arthur's grandmother
Arthur's grandfather
Arthur's cousin
Arthur's cousin
Arthur's cousin
Arthur's friend
Arthur's friend

B Cue slips

Bertha's father
Bertha's mother
Bertha's sister
Bertha's brother
Bertha's aunt
Bertha's uncle
Bertha's brother-in-law
Bertha's sister-in-law
Bertha's niece
Bertha's nephew
Bertha's grandmother
Bertha's grandfather
Bertha's cousin
Bertha's cousin
Bertha's cousin
Bertha's friend
Bertha's friend

Shopping for and Preparing Food
Teacher's Notes and Activity Sheets

Activity Title	■ Activity Type	Page
Shopping Carts on the Shelves? Students look at a supermarket scene in the Dictionary and respond to a series of yes/no questions.	■ Silent Drill	16
Cooking with Carla Students listen to a chef narrating a cooking show and point to the correct pictures in the Dictionary.	■ Listen and Point	17
A Bottle, A Carton, A Jar Students listen to a woman preparing a shopping list and circle the correct containers.	■ Listen and Circle	18
How Much Do You Save? Students complete identical coupons by asking for and giving information on savings, quantity, and expiration date.	■ Information Gap	19
Food Survey Students exchange and record information about food likes and dislikes and compile a class survey.	■ Interview	20
What Do We Need to Buy? Students plan a meal and create a shopping list by working with ingredients they have in their kitchens.	■ Cooperative Jigsaw	21
Food Go Around Students move markers around a game board while answering questions and demonstrating knowledge about food.	■ Board Game	22
Fruit Salad for 30 Students plan and make a fruit salad and write a description of the experience.	■ Language Experience	23

Reproducible activity sheets on pages 25–28.

Shopping Carts on the Shelves?

Focus: Identifying items in a supermarket.

Materials: Answer Cards and Don't Look Mask, p. 179; **The Supermarket, Dictionary, pp. 14–15.**

Before class, duplicate and cut apart a class set of the Answer Cards and Don't Look Mask. Look over the silent drill questions and the target vocabulary (step 4 below).

Preview

1. Hold up a set of answer cards and tell students that they will be listening to and answering a series of questions by raising the correct answer card.
2. Direct students to open their dictionaries to pages 14 and 15. Ask students to imagine that they are in the supermarket. Talk about what they are doing (looking at frozen foods in the freezer, pushing a shopping cart down the aisle).

Presentation

3. Distribute the answer cards and masks. Have students cover the vocabulary at the bottom of the page and listen to your questions about the picture. Ask the first question: "Are there *customers* in this supermarket?" Tell students to raise the Yes card if the answer is yes, the No card if it is no, and the Not Sure card when there's not enough information to answer yes or no. Get class consensus on the first answer before continuing.

Practice (with Answers)

4. Ask the following questions:
   Are there *customers* in this supermarket? (Yes)
   Are there *frozen foods* in the *freezer?* (Yes)
   Are there *canned goods* on the floor? (No)
   Are there tired *cashiers* in this supermarket? (Not Sure)
   Are there *shopping carts* on the *shelves?* (No)
   Are there *cash registers* near the *checkout counter?* (Yes)
   Are there *groceries* in the *shopping basket?* (Yes)
   Are there *baked goods* on the *shelves?* (Yes)
   Are there delicious *snacks* in this supermarket? (Not Sure)
   Are there *beverages* in the *produce* section? (No)

Follow-up

5. Have students use the supermarket dictionary pages to talk about food-shopping habits and preferences. Ask students to share information about where they shop (convenience store, local grocer, supermarket) and describe a typical trip to the market.

Cooking with Carla

Focus: Identifying food preparation tasks.

Materials: Don't Look Mask, p. 179; listening cassette; **Kitchen Verbs, Dictionary, p. 31.**

Before class, duplicate a class set of the Don't Look Mask. Look over the target vocabulary in the tapescript below.

Preview

1. Tell students that they will be listening to "Chef Carla" describe various tasks in the kitchen.
2. Direct students to open their dictionaries to page 31. Have students find the following foods: potato, carrot, and steak. Ask the class to identify several ways of preparing each food (cut/slice the carrot, bake/fry the potato). Write students' suggestions on the board and add any target vocabulary that is missing.

Presentation

3. Distribute the masks and have students cover the vocabulary at the bottom of the page. Tell students to listen to the tape and to point to the correct pictures in their dictionaries. Assure students that they will have several opportunities to hear the listening passage.
4. Play the tape through "Never use a dull one!" Stop the tape and check to be sure that students are pointing to picture #6. Replay this section of the tape until all students are pointing to picture #6.

Practice

5. Play the tape, stopping when necessary. Replay the tape two to five times.

Follow-up

6. Check for comprehension of the target vocabulary by asking student volunteers to imagine that they're in the kitchen. Have them form sentences, such as "I'm carving a turkey," "I'm beating an egg." Students can respond by saying or pointing to the numbers associated with each picture.

Variation

To make the follow-up more challenging, have students describe how they prepare a meal. Ask individual students to take the role of chef and share their food preparation procedures with the class.

Tapescript (with Answers)

Listen to Chef Carla describe how to prepare a meal. Point to the correct pictures.

Welcome to our show, "Cooking with Carla." I'm your host Carla Childs, and today we'll review some cooking basics. Remember, cooking is easy if you have good food, good kitchen equipment, and good techniques. Now, let's begin with our beautiful roast turkey. Do you see it? Always *carve (6)* your turkey with a sharp knife. Never use a dull one!* Next, take two carrots and *grate (2)* them into small pieces. Always use fresh carrots for your stuffing!* Use a clean cutting board and *slice (10)* an onion. You'll need two or three slices. Oh, excuse me. Onions make me cry.* You can use the same knife to *chop (11)* the onion into tiny pieces. But watch your fingers!* Next, take four eggs and *break (7)* them into a mixing bowl. Use both hands, please!* Now you are ready to *beat (8)* the eggs. A beater like mine works well, but you can also use a fork.* Let's see. . .oh, it's time to check our broccoli in that large double pot. I usually *steam (12)* it for, oh, eight or nine minutes. Put on the cover—we don't want to lose those vitamins!* Let's make another side dish in a small pot. Do you see it? Oh, dear, don't *boil (16)* the rice—lower the heat please!* If you want, substitute delicious french fries for the rice. *Fry (15)* them in a pan with a little oil. Don't they look wonderful?* A fresh green salad will taste good with our meal. Do you see how I *peel (5)* this cucumber? Hold it carefully and work away from your body.* Finally, we're ready for our beverages. Please hold your glass steady when you *pour (4)* the milk—we don't want a mess in the kitchen!* Remember to serve both coffee and tea, and don't forget the sugar and cream. You'll need extra spoons to *stir (1)* those drinks.* Oh, dear, I almost forgot about dessert! Well, look at the fantastic cake I've prepared. *Bake (14)* it in the oven at 375 degrees for 45 minutes and always use pot holders! Oops! Well, that's all for now! Bon appétit and bye-bye!

A Bottle, A Carton, A Jar

Focus: Identifying containers for grocery items.

Materials: Activity sheet, p. 25; Don't Look Mask, p. 179; listening cassette; **Containers, Quantities, and Money, Dictionary, pp. 12–13.**

Before class, duplicate a class set of the activity sheet and the Don't Look Mask. Look over the target vocabulary in the tapescript below.

Preview

1. Tell students that they will be listening for items on a shopping list.
2. Direct students to open their dictionaries to pages 12 and 13 and to look over the pictures. Distribute the masks and have students cover the vocabulary at the bottom of the page. Ask students to name the container as you point to or identify each picture, "Look at #1. How do you buy milk?"

Presentation

3. Copy number 1 (the example) from the activity sheet onto the board. Explain the task to students, and assure them that they will have several opportunities to hear the listening passage.
4. Play the tape through number 1 "We're out of eggs, so pick up a. . . ." Stop the tape and review the example on the board.
5. Distribute the activity sheets and review the directions.

Practice

6. Play the tape, stopping after each item. When necessary, replay each item two to five times.
7. Have students, in pairs, listen to the tape again. Circulate as students check their answers with each other. Replay the tape to clarify any problems.

Follow-up

8. Have student pairs create their own shopping lists using the vocabulary on pages 12 and 13 as a guide. Encourage students to include items that they usually buy. One student can dictate the list as the other writes down the items. Students then reverse roles.

Variation

To make this activity more challenging, ask students to form groups of four in order to brainstorm as many items as they can for each container. Then have the class create a list of ways to reuse the containers.

Tapescript (with Answers)

Listen to the woman preparing a shopping list. Circle the correct container for each item.

1. Wait a minute, Sara! I know you're in a hurry, but I need a few things at the market. Here's my shopping list. Can you read it? We're out of eggs, so pick up a . . . . *(carton)*
2. While you're in the dairy section, could you get some butter? This recipe says I need only one . . . . *(stick)*
3. Potato chips? No, we have enough junk food in this house! Well, we are having a barbecue on Sunday. OK, just one . . . . *(bag)*
4. Hmmm. There are a few more things. I think we need some bread for sandwiches. Could you get a . . . . *(loaf)*
5. Oh, I almost forgot to give you this coupon for tuna fish. If we buy two, we can get a free . . . . *(can)*
6. Here's another coupon for spaghetti. My favorite brand, too. It's for 25 cents off a . . . . *(box)*
7. Let's see, what else do we need? We have to wrap all those sandwiches. We're low on aluminum foil. Just get one . . . . *(roll)*
8. Oh, and don't forget my favorite diet soda. No, I don't want a bottle, get me cans. How many? Oh, I guess one . . . . *(six-pack)*

How Much Do You Save?

Focus: Asking for and giving information about coupons.

Materials: Activity sheet, p. 26; manila folders (one per pair); newspaper coupons (two per student); **Containers, Quantities, and Money, Dictionary, pp. 12–13.**

Before class, duplicate half a class set of the activity sheet. Cut apart the A and B sections of the sheets and keep them separate. Copy the questions from the activity sheet onto the board.

Preview

1. Tell students that they will be working in pairs to find out the missing information on grocery coupons.
2. Direct students to open their dictionaries to pages 12 and 13. Ask students to locate an item that they have bought with a coupon. Ask students what kind of information can be found on a coupon, such as name of product, expiration date, size or quantity, and monetary value. Draw a rectangle on the board and create a coupon according to students' directions.

Presentation

3. Use the questions on the board to model the language and clarification strategies you want students to use in the activity. Have the class practice asking and answering the questions using the drawing of the coupon on the board.
4. Pair students and assign each one an A or a B role. Explain to students that they will each have coupons with some information missing. Point out that the missing information is on their partner's coupons. Tell students that they will take turns asking for and giving the missing information in order to complete their coupons.
5. Distribute a manila folder to each pair, to be propped up between the students as a

screen. Distribute the A and B activity sheets to the appropriate partners. Review the directions and instruct students to look only at their own papers and not at their partner's.
6. Tell students to look at the example on their coupons and tell you the name of the product. Check comprehension by asking A students, "When does the coupon for Roma tomatoes expire?" Ask B students, "How much do you save on Roma tomatoes?"
7. Have one pair demonstrate the activity by asking for and giving information about coupon #1. Remind students to look only at their own coupons.

Practice

8. Have students, in pairs, ask and answer questions about the missing information on their coupons. Once they complete the task, partners can compare coupons to be sure they are the same.

Follow-up

9. Have pairs form groups of four to generate a shopping list, using dictionary pages 6–13. Distribute eight coupons to each group. Have students see which coupons they can use, and search for groups who want to exchange or "swap" coupons.

Food Survey

Focus: Discussing food likes and dislikes.

Materials: Activity sheet, p. 25; **Vegetables, Fruits,** and **Meat, Poultry, and Seafood, Dictionary, pp. 6–11.**

Before class, duplicate a class set of the activity sheet.

Preview

1. Tell students that they will be interviewing their classmates and talking about foods they like and dislike.
2. Direct students to open their dictionaries to pages 6 and 7. Write the following three categories on the board: Vegetable Soup, Fruit Salad, Main Dish. Ask students what different vegetables they would choose to prepare a soup. Write the suggested vegetable names on the board. Refer students to pages 8–11, and follow the same procedure for the other two categories.

Presentation

3. Copy the grid from the activity sheet onto the board. Model the questions from the grid: "What kind of fruit do you like?"; "What vegetable do you dislike?"; and so on. Using the grid on the board, write your name in the first column and have the class ask you the first question. Answer the question about yourself and write your answer in the grid box. Explain that only short answers are written in the boxes below the questions.
4. Ask a volunteer to come to the board. Write the student's name under your name on the grid. Have different students ask the volunteer one question each from the grid. Write the answers on the grid.

Practice

5. Divide the class into groups of four and distribute an activity sheet to each student.
6. Have students take turns asking the questions of the person on their left, while the other group members listen and write the answers on their grids. When students have completed their grids, they can use the information to talk about the discussion questions below the grid.
7. Set a 20-minute time limit for students to complete the task. Circulate and monitor group practice.

Follow-up

8. Use the grid on the board to elicit responses from each group. Number the groups and write the group numbers in the first column. Ask the survey questions and write the groups' responses on the board. Continue asking the groups all the questions, writing the single majority response wherever possible. If each group member has a different answer, write "varies."
9. When you've finished interviewing all the groups, have students use your completed survey to comment on patterns in the class.

Variation

To make this activity easier, conduct a teacher-directed survey with the whole class.

What Do We Need to Buy?

Focus: Planning a meal and creating a shopping list.

Materials: Activity sheet, p. 25; Picture Cards #1–#20, p. 180; four 8-1/2" × 11" sheets of blank paper; large newsprint sheets (one per four students, plus one extra); markers (one per four students); **Containers, Quantities, and Money, Dictionary, pp. 12–13.**

Before class, duplicate the activity sheet (one per four students). Cut apart the numbered cue cards on the sheets and keep them separate. Collect the newsprint sheets and markers. Write the heading "Shopping List" on each newsprint sheet. Draw the following food items on the four 8-1/2" × 11" sheets of paper (one picture per sheet): an onion, a tomato, a chicken, mushrooms. Use Picture Cards #1, #17, #18, and #20, p. 180 for reference.

Preview

1. Tell students that they will be planning menus and making shopping lists.
2. Direct students to open their dictionaries to pages 12 and 13. Announce "I have friends coming for dinner and I have all the food on these pages in my kitchen. What can I make?" Have students suggest a main dish, side dish, dessert, and beverage, and write the menu on the board. Next, use the following conversation to elicit food items not featured on the dictionary page: A: What else do I need to buy? B: Wine. A: A bottle of wine? B: OK.

Presentation

3. Invite four volunteers to the front of the room. Give each one an 8-1/2" x 11" food picture. Tell the volunteers to conceal their pictures from the class. Explain that each picture represents a food item in their kitchen. Tell the class to listen carefully in order to help plan a meal based on the food mentioned. Have the volunteers describe their food to the class without revealing their pictures. Ask the class to think of a special dish that all four students could make using the available food items.
4. Post one of the newsprint "shopping lists" on the board. Have students call out the names of food items needed to prepare the special dish. Ask a volunteer to record the items on the shopping list. Point out that perfect spelling is not necessary.

Practice

5. Have students form groups of four and number off 1–4 within each group. Ask each group to choose a recorder. Distribute the appropriate numbered cue card to each student, and a marker and a shopping list to each recorder. Explain that groups must agree on a dinner menu that uses as many items as possible from their "kitchens" before they compile a shopping list of additional foods. Tell the recorders to write down both the group's menu and the items for the shopping list.
6. Set a 20-minute time limit for students to complete the activity. Circulate and monitor group practice.

Follow-up

7. Post the completed shopping lists and talk about the different food choices and the most original menu.

Variations

To make the practice easier, distribute one picture card (#1–#20) from p. 180 to each pair. Determine the food items in the class's "kitchen," and have the class brainstorm a menu and write a shopping list. (See step 4 above.)

To make the follow-up more challenging have each group categorize their shopping lists by market sections. Use dictionary pages 14–15 as a reference.

Food Go Around

Focus: Demonstrating knowledge of food.

Materials: Activity sheet, p. 27; Picture Cards #1–#20, p. 180; coins (one per group); scratch paper; four 8-1/2" x 11" sheets of blank paper; paper clips; **Vegetables, Fruits,** and **Meat, Poultry, and Seafood, Dictionary, pp. 6–11.**

Before class, duplicate the activity sheet (one per four students). Duplicate the picture cards (one set per four students). Cut apart the picture cards and clip them together in sets. Draw the following pictures on the 8-1/2" x 11" sheets of paper: mushrooms, a ham, apples, and a fish. Use Picture Cards #2, #4, #7, and #20, p. 180 for reference.

Preview

1. Tell students that they are going to test their knowledge of food by playing a board game with their classmates.
2. Direct students to open their dictionaries to pages 6 and 7. Write the following statements and questions on the board: "Say it and spell it," "How do you buy it?" "Tell how you prepare it," and "Do you like it?" Ask the class to choose one vegetable from pages 6 and 7 and to respond to each statement or question on the board.

Presentation

3. Copy the activity sheet onto the board, filling in only the first four squares. Put the 8-1/2" x 11" food pictures on the chalk ledge, face down. Invite three volunteers to the front of the room. Have the volunteers write their names on separate pieces of scratch paper while you do the same. Tape these papers to the "Start" square. Explain that these are the game markers.
4. Show the class a coin and demonstrate flipping it "heads" and "tails." Flip the coin

and move your marker on the board, one space for heads, two spaces for tails. Move your marker to the square "Pick a card: Say it and spell it" or "Name a food you buy for a salad." Have the class read the directions aloud. Follow the directions. Play two rounds of the game with the three volunteers. Get class consensus on the accuracy of the volunteers' responses. Point out that when a response is not correct, the player cannot flip the coin on her next turn and must answer the same question again.

Practice

5. Divide the class into groups of four. Distribute the activity sheets (game boards), picture card sets, coins, and scratch paper to each group. Have each group create four "markers" and place them on the "Start" square.
6. Check for general understanding of the game by asking yes/no questions, such as "Do I move two spaces for heads?" and "Do I pick a card from the top of the pile?"
7. Set a 20-minute time limit for the game and begin play.
8. Circulate and monitor student practice. (In cases where groups cannot come to consensus, you serve as referee.)

Follow-up

9. Divide the class into two teams, A and B. Copy the activity sheet onto the board, replacing the directions with numbers. Have team members take turns flipping coins and answering your questions (the original questions or new ones).

Variation

Divide the class into groups of five. Students 1 and 2 form team A, students 3 and 4 form team B, and student 5 serves as the referee. Proceed as before (step 9). Allow referees to use the dictionary and other resources to decide if spelling and other responses are accurate.

Fruit Salad for 30

Preview (Day 1)

1. Tell students that they will be working in groups to make a fruit salad according to a recipe.
2. Direct students to turn to pages 8 and 9 in their dictionaries. Ask students what fruits they like or dislike, and how they buy them: one by one, by the bunch, by the pound, or by the bag.
3. Divide students into groups of four and distribute the Day 1 section of the activity sheet. Review the directions on the sheet with the class. Have each member of the group take turns asking and answering the questions on the activity sheet. Allow time for the group to decide on the fruits they'd like to use in a fruit salad. Ask each student to bring one piece of fruit to class the next day.

Presentation (Day 2)

4. Pantomime the verbs from the recipe on the activity sheet, such as peel, cut, slice, or chop. See if students can guess what you're doing. Refer students to page 31 in their dictionaries to confirm their guesses.
5. Collect all the fruit from the students and ask two volunteers to wash it off and bring it to the front of the class.
6. Have students re-form their groups from the day before, then distribute the Day 2 activity sheet. Have each group choose a "head chef" to oversee the fruit salad preparation.
7. Have the head chefs assist you as you demonstrate the various steps in the recipe.
8. Have students, in their groups, read over the recipe and decide who will do each step. Ask students to notice the utensils and other ingredients they will need.

Practice

9. When all the students have read the recipe and decided upon their different tasks, ask the head chefs to pick up their supplies from you. Remind students that they need to prepare the salad according to the recipe and to follow all the directions. Then have the groups proceed with the activity.
10. Circulate to help all students participate in the activity. Encourage students to come to you if they need assistance.

Follow-up

11. When the activity is finished, ask the groups to share their fruit salads. Compare flavors, textures, and appearances.
12. Have students put their recipes away. Elicit the recipe for the salad from students by asking questions, such as "What do you do first?" and "What do you do to the apples?" Write the recipe on the board exactly as the students tell it to you. Have students read the recipe aloud and copy it.

   The following is a typical level-one recipe: Making fruit salad. First wash and clean fruit. Peel it. Chop the apples. Slice bananas and put all the fruit in bowl. You can put in yogurt. Stir every fruit. The salad is delicious.

Your Notes

A Bottle, A Carton, A Jar (See Teacher's Notes, page 18.)

■ Listen to the woman preparing a shopping list.
■ Circle the correct container for each item.

1. bottle (carton) jar
2. stick tube bag
3. loaf bag book
4. can loaf stick

5. tub bottle can
6. box tube stick
7. stick roll bar
8. six-pack loaf jar

---✀

Food Survey (See Teacher's Notes, page 20.)

■ Take turns asking and answering the questions about different foods.
■ Record your classmate's answers on the grid.

NAME	What kind of fruit do you...?		What kind of vegetable do you...?		What kind of meat or poultry do you...?		What kind of seafood do you...?	
	☺	☹	☺	☹	☺	☹	☺	☹

■ After you complete the grid, discuss these questions with your group:
  Is there a difference between men's and women's answers?
  Is there a fruit, vegetable, meat, poultry, or seafood that's popular in your group?

---✀

What Do We Need to Buy? (See Teacher's Notes, page 21.)

#1

#2

#3

#4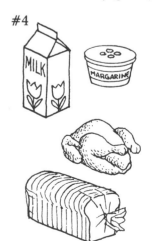

How Much Do You Save? (See Teacher's Notes, page 19.)

- Look at the coupons below.
- Take turns asking your partner these kinds of questions:
    How much do you save with this coupon?
    How much do you need to buy?
    When does this coupon expire?
- Write in the missing information.
- When you don't hear an answer, ask "How much?" or "When?"

A

B

- Look at the coupons below.
- Take turns asking your partner these kinds of questions:
    How much do you save with this coupon?
    How much do you need to buy?
    When does this coupon expire?
- Write in the missing information.
- When you don't hear an answer, ask "How much?" or "When?"

Food Go Around (See Teacher's Notes, page 22.)

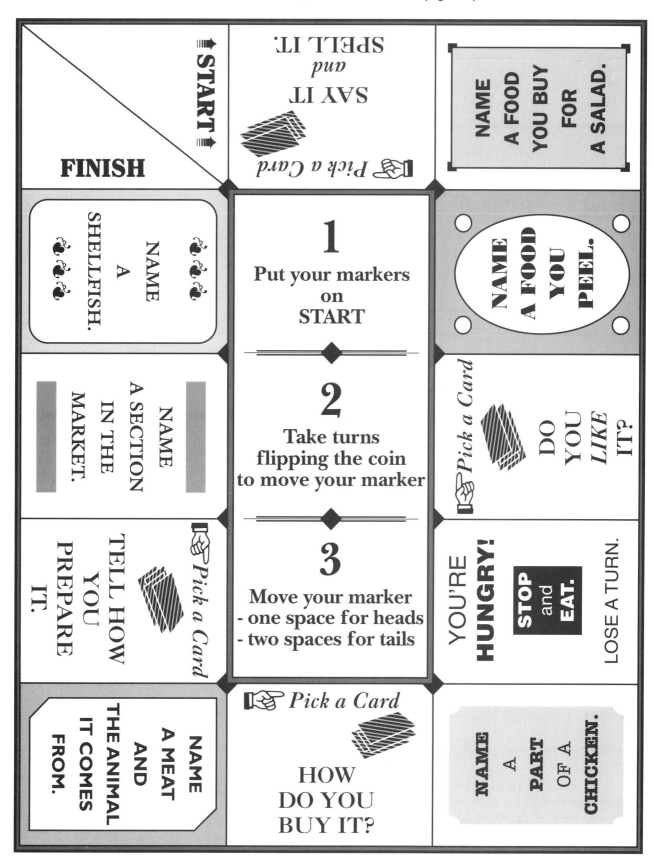

START

☞ Pick a Card

SAY IT and SPELL IT.

NAME A FOOD YOU BUY FOR A SALAD.

FINISH

NAME A SHELLFISH.

1
Put your markers on START

NAME A FOOD YOU PEEL.

NAME A SECTION IN THE MARKET.

2
Take turns flipping the coin to move your marker

☞ Pick a Card
DO YOU LIKE IT?

☞ Pick a Card
TELL HOW YOU PREPARE IT.

3
Move your marker
- one space for heads
- two spaces for tails

YOU'RE HUNGRY!
STOP and EAT.
LOSE A TURN.

NAME A MEAT AND THE ANIMAL IT COMES FROM.

☞ Pick a Card
HOW DO YOU BUY IT?

NAME A PART OF A CHICKEN.

Fruit Salad for 30 (See Teacher's Notes, page 23.)

Day 1

- Write your classmates' names on the grids below.
- Ask "Do you like . . . ?" for grid #1, and "Do you have a . . . ?" for #2.
- Make a check (√) under the fruits each person likes.
- Make a check (√) under the utensils each person has.

NAME	APPLES	ORANGES	BANANAS	PEARS	PEACHES	GRAPES	OTHER

NAME	BOWL	BIG SPOON	SMALL KNIFE	COLANDER	CUTTING BOARD

---✂

Day 2

- Collect your supplies from the teacher.
- Prepare your fruit salad with your group.

Recipe

1. Wash and dry the fruit.
2. Peel the bananas and oranges.
3. Separate and cut up the orange sections.
4. Slice the bananas.
5. Slice and chop the apples.
6. Slice or chop any other fruit.
7. Put all the fruit into a bowl and pour yogurt on it.
8. Do you have any raisins or nuts? Put them in the bowl too.
9. Mix everything together.
10. Serve the salad and eat it!

Serving Food and Dining Out
Teacher's Notes and Activity Sheets

The Food's Delicious Here!

Focus: Identifying activities in a restaurant.
Materials: Answer Cards and Don't Look Mask, p. 179; **Family Restaurant and Cocktail Lounge, Dictionary, p. 16.**

Before class, duplicate and cut apart a class set of the Answer Cards and Don't Look Mask. Look over the silent drill questions and the target vocabulary (step 4 below).

Preview

1. Hold up a set of answer cards and tell students that they will be listening to and answering a series of questions by raising the correct answer card.
2. Direct students to open their dictionaries to page 16. Ask students to identify the people in the restaurant (waitress, cook, couple, family) and talk about what they are doing.

Presentation

3. Distribute the answer cards and masks. Have students cover the lower picture on the page and listen to your questions about the upper picture. Ask the first question: "Is this a *family restaurant?*" Tell students to raise the Yes card if the answer is yes, the No card if it is no, and the Not Sure card when there's not enough information to answer yes or no. Get class consensus on the first answer before continuing.

Practice (with Answers)

4. Ask the following questions:
Is this a *family restaurant?* (Yes)
Is the *waiter* standing and holding a *menu?* (Yes)
Are the people at the table using the *ketchup?* (No)
Is the *cook* in the kitchen? (Yes)
Are the *sandwiches* at this restaurant delicious? (Not sure)
Is the man on the far left drinking *tea?* (No)
Is the *busboy* going into the kitchen? (Yes)
Is the *waitress* talking to the busboy? (No)
Is the little girl sitting in a *high chair?* (Yes)
Is the couple on the left sitting in a *booth?* (Yes)
Is the couple on the left listening to music on the *jukebox?* (Not sure)

Follow-up

5. Ask students to identify the people in the restaurant and what each person is saying. Have the class talk about the conversations that might be taking place.

Lunch at Chasson's

> **Focus:** Identifying activities in a restaurant.
>
> **Materials:** Don't Look Mask, p. 179; listening cassette; **Restaurant Verbs, Dictionary, p. 17.**
>
> ---
>
> *Before class, duplicate a class set of the Don't Look Mask. Look over the target vocabulary in the tapescript below.*

Preview

1. Tell students that they will be listening to the manager of a restaurant talk about the people working and dining there.
2. Direct students to open their dictionaries to page 17. Mime two or three of the actions depicted on the page and have students guess what you're doing. Then invite three volunteers to come to the front of the room and have each mime a different action (setting the table, taking an order, serving). Tell the class to point to the corresponding pictures.

Presentation

3. Distribute the masks and have students cover the vocabulary at the bottom of the page. Tell students to listen to the tape and to point to the correct pictures in their dictionaries. Assure students that they will have several opportunities to hear the listening passage.
4. Play the tape through "Luis always forgets the fork when he *sets* the table." Stop the tape and check to be sure that students are pointing to picture #8. Replay this section of the tape until all students are pointing to picture #8.

Practice

5. Play the tape, stopping when necessary. Replay the tape two to five times.

Follow-up

6. Check for comprehension of the target vocabulary by asking questions, such as "Where is the waitress who's serving a sandwich?" Students can respond by saying "#3" or pointing to the correct picture.

Variation

To make the follow-up more challenging, have student groups write a story based on the dictionary page. Replay the tape whenever students want to clarify something they've heard.

Tapescript (with Answers)

Listen to Georges Chasson talk about his restaurant. Point to the items or people you hear Georges talking about.

Welcome to Chasson's. We're having a busy afternoon. Louis— he's the busboy in the red vest—do you see him? He's *setting (8)* a table. He's putting the napkin on the left and the knife on the right. Louis always forgets the fork when he *sets (8)* the table.* Oh, and there's our cook, Pierre, in the kitchen. Pierre's *cooking (4)* his specialty: soup du jour. He *cooks (4)* very well.* Mrs. Feldman is *ordering (5)* from the menu. Her table has flowers, a glass, and a napkin, but no fork! She's *ordering (5)* lunch and some silverware!* At the next table, Rashid is *clearing (6)* the dishes. Rashid is a new busboy, but he *clears (6)* the tables quickly.* Monica, our new waitress, is next to Louis. She's *giving (9)* Mr. Simms a menu, but Mr. Simms always gets the same thing for lunch. See? Monica is *taking (10)* the menu back because Mr. Simms doesn't need to look at it.* Our waitress Hilda is *serving (3)* a customer a sandwich. Hilda's the one in the blue uniform. She's always friendly when she *serves (3)* lunch.* Oh, no! Wanda is *burning (14)* the paella! She's helping in the kitchen today, but she always *burns (14)* everything.* Ah, there's a nice young man *drinking (2)* a glass of milk. And there's a nice young woman *eating (1)* a salad. I wonder if they are together.* Our cashier, Julia, is the older woman with the glasses. Do you see the customer *paying (7)* her? All the customers *pay (7)* Julia before they leave.* Oh, no! A customer is *holding (12)* up his fork. I hope it isn't dirty . . . Louis, can I speak with you for a moment?

What'll Ya Have?

Focus: Listening for orders in a coffee shop.

Materials: Activity sheet, p. 39; listening cassette; **Common Prepared Foods, Dictionary, p. 18.**

Before class, duplicate a class set of the activity sheet. Look over the target vocabulary in the tapescript below.

Preview

1. Tell students that they will be listening for orders in a coffee shop.
2. Direct students to open their dictionaries to page 18 and look over the target vocabulary. Write these categories on the board: Main Dishes, Side Dishes, Beverages, and Desserts. Elicit items for each category from the class and write the students' "menu" on the board.
3. Use the menu from step 2 to review the language of ordering food: "I'd like an order of fries." "I'd like a hamburger with ketchup." Have students practice ordering the items from the menu.

Presentation

4. Copy number 1 (the example) from the activity sheet onto the board. Review the food names and abbreviations (S,M,L,w/) under the four categories. Explain the task to students, and assure them that they will have several opportunities to hear the listening passage.
5. Play the tape through number 1 "Oh, and an order of *fries,* too." Stop the tape and review the example on the board.
6. Distribute the activity sheets and review the directions.

Practice

7. Play the tape, stopping after each customer completes an order. When necessary, replay each order two to five times.
8. Elicit students' responses for each order and get class consensus on the accuracy of the responses. Replay the tape to clarify any problems.

Follow-up

9. Teach students clarification questions for this situation, such as "What size cola? Small, medium, or large?" and "Do you want your burger with ketchup or mustard?"
10. Pair students and have them take turns giving and writing down orders for food. Use the activity sheet or page 18 in the dictionary as a menu. One student orders and the other writes. Then students can reverse roles.

Tapescript (with Answers)

Listen to the people ordering food in a coffee shop. Circle the correct items in each order.
1. Hello, I'd like a *hamburger with ketchup,* a *small salad,* and a *large cola.* Oh, and an order of *fries,* too.
2. Please give me an order of *fried chicken.* I love the chicken here. I'd like some *mashed potatoes* and a *small salad* with that. And I'd like *coffee, black.* No cream, no sugar.
3. We'd like a *pepperoni pizza,* a *small salad,* a *small cola,* and a *medium cola.* Our son will have a *hamburger with mustard, french fries,* and a small, no I'm sorry, *a large milk.* He needs to drink more milk!
4. Could I get a *taco*—a *chicken taco,* a *hot dog with ketchup and mustard,* a cup of coffee with cream, no, no coffee, just some *tea with lemon.* The doctor says no more coffee for me!
5. I'll have the *fried chicken,* my wife will have the *beef taco,* and the kids will have a *cheese pizza.* We'd like *french fries,* a *medium cola,* a *small milk,* one *tea with lemon,* and one *coffee with cream.* Did you get that?

What's on the Menu?

Focus: Asking for and giving prices on a menu.

Materials: Activity sheet, p. 40; manila folders (one per pair); large sheets of newsprint (one per four students); markers (one per four students); **Common Prepared Foods, Dictionary, p. 18.**

Before class, duplicate half a class set of the activity sheet. Cut apart the A and B sections of the sheets and keep them separate. Copy the conversation from the activity sheet onto the board.

Preview

1. Tell students that they will be working in pairs to find out the missing prices on a menu.
2. Have students brainstorm the names of different sandwiches. List the names on the board as a "menu." Ask students to give you a price for each sandwich. Write these prices on the "menu."

Presentation

3. Use the conversation on the board to model the language and clarification strategy you want students to use in the activity. Have the class practice the conversation, substituting different sandwich names.
4. Pair students and assign each one an A or a B role. Explain to students that they will each have a menu with different prices missing. Point out that the missing information is on their partner's menu. Tell students that they will take turns asking for and giving the missing prices in order to complete their menus.

5. Distribute a manila folder to each pair, to be propped up between the students as a screen. Distribute the A and B activity sheets to the appropriate partners. Review the directions and instruct students to look only at their own papers and not at their partner's.
6. Tell students to look at the example on their menus and tell you the price of a chicken sandwich. Check comprehension by asking A students, "How much is a roast beef sandwich?" Ask B students, "How much is a cheese sandwich?"
7. Have one pair demonstrate the activity by asking for and giving prices from their menus. Remind students to look only at their own menus.

Practice

8. Have students, in pairs, ask and answer questions about the missing prices on their menus. Once they complete the task, partners can compare menus to be sure they are the same.

Follow-up

9. Have pairs form groups of four. Direct the groups to look at page 18 in their dictionaries. Explain that each group will create a restaurant menu using the target vocabulary on the page. Distribute large sheets of newsprint and markers to each group. Circulate during the group work and post the resulting menus around the room.

Set the Table

> **Focus:** Giving and following directions for setting a table.
>
> **Materials:** Activity sheet, p. 41; two 8-1/2" x 11" sheets of blank paper; manila folders (one per pair); scratch paper; a place setting including a plate, glass, cup, napkin, fork, knife, and spoon; **The Dining Room, Dictionary, p. 29.**
>
> ---
>
> *Before class, duplicate half a class set of the activity sheet. Cut apart table settings 1, 2, 3, and 4 and keep them separate. Draw an enlarged version of place setting #1 on both of the 8-1/2" x 11" sheets of paper. Collect half a class set of manila folders. Gather the realia for the place setting.*

Preview

1. Tell students that they will be drawing place settings according to their partner's directions.
2. Direct students to open their dictionaries to page 29. Discuss the location of the items on the table: "Where's the fork?" "It's next to the plate, on the left."
3. Have students tell you how to set a table like the one pictured in the dictionary. As students direct you ("Put the plate in the center."), carry out their directions using the realia, or draw the place setting on the board. Incorporate appropriate clarification questions as you respond to the directions, such as "Where?"; "Next to what?"; or "On the right or on the left?"
4. Invite a volunteer to the board to draw a place setting according to your directions. Be sure to modify the place setting from the one you drew in step 3.

Presentation

5. Ask two of your more advanced students to come to the board. Call one student the "manager" and the other the "busperson." Give the busperson a piece of chalk and the manager one of the 8-1/2" x 11" copies of place setting #1. Have the manager use the picture to tell the busperson how to draw a table setting on the board. Show the other 8-1/2" x 11" place setting to the class so that the rest of the students know what the manager is looking at. Encourage the class to help the busperson and manager complete their tasks.

Practice

6. Pair students and identify one as manager, the other as busperson. Distribute a manila folder to each pair, to be propped up between the students as a screen. Explain that the managers will give directions and the buspeople will draw what they hear. Stress that correct placement of the items, rather than quality of the artwork, is the goal of the activity.
7. Give place setting #1 to the managers and scratch paper to the buspeople. While pairs work on the first place setting, circulate and monitor their progress. When partners finish, they can compare pictures and talk about any discrepancies.
8. After the pairs compare place setting #1, have them pick up place setting #2 and repeat the activity. When partners finish #2, ask them to compare pictures, switch roles, and pick up place settings #3 and #4 and additional scratch paper.

Follow-up

9. Divide the class into several teams. (Each row could be a team.) Give the first person on each team a blank sheet of paper and call out the first direction: "Draw a plate in the center." Have the first person draw the plate and pass the paper to the next person on the team. Continue giving directions until all team members have had a turn. Have the last student on each team show the team's drawing. Compare drawings and repeat the activity.

Dining Survey

Focus: Discussing dining preferences.

Materials: Activity sheet, p. 41;
Common Prepared Foods, Dictionary,
p. 18.

_Before class, duplicate a class set of
the activity sheet._

Preview

1. Tell students that they will be interviewing
   their classmates and talking about food
   preferences.
2. Direct students to open their dictionaries
   to page 18. Ask students to name local
   restaurants where they could find the foods
   shown on the page. Write students'
   suggestions on the board.

Presentation

3. Copy the grid from the activity sheet onto
   the board. Model the questions from the
   grid: "What's your favorite kind of food?";
   "How often do you go to restaurants?"; and
   so on. Using the grid on the board, write
   your name in the first column and have the
   class ask you the first question. Answer the
   question about yourself and write your
   answer in the grid box. Explain that only
   short answers are written in the boxes below
   the questions.
4. Ask a volunteer to come to the board. Write
   the student's name under your name on the
   grid. Have different students ask the
   volunteer one question each from the grid.
   Write the answers on the grid.

Practice

5. Divide the class into groups of five and
   distribute an activity sheet to each student.
6. Have students take turns asking the
   questions of the person on their left while
   the other group members listen and write
   the answers on their grids. When students
   have completed their grids, they can use the
   information to talk about the discussion
   questions below the grid.
7. Set a 20-minute time limit for students to
   complete the task. Circulate and monitor
   student practice.

Follow-up

8. Use the grid on the board to elicit responses
   from each group. Number the groups and
   write the group numbers in the first column.
   Ask the survey questions and write the
   groups' responses on the board. Continue
   asking the groups all the questions, writing
   the single majority response wherever
   possible. If each group member has
   a different answer, write "varies."
9. When you've finished interviewing all the
   groups, have students use your completed
   survey to comment on patterns in the class.

Variations

To make this activity easier, conduct a
teacher-directed survey with the whole class.

To make this activity more challenging,
have groups generate three additional items
to include in their surveys.

It's a Party!

Focus: Describing a sequence of events at a party.

Materials: Activity sheet, p. 42; four 8-1/2" x 11" blank sheets of paper; Picture Cards #131–#134, p. 186; paper clips; **Restaurant Verbs, Dictionary, p. 17.**

Before class, duplicate the activity sheet (one per six students). Cut apart the pictures, scramble each set, and clip the sets together. Copy the following drawings from the Picture Cards onto the 8-1/2" x 11" sheets of paper (one drawing per sheet): cook, serve, eat, and clean. On the copy of picture card #134, in the hand of the figure, draw a plate with a piece of cake. Write the numbers 1–4 across the board.

Preview

1. Tell students that they will be working in groups to sequence pictures that tell the story of a party.
2. Elicit descriptions of the things people do before and during a party: clean the house, cook, set the table, serve, and so on. Write students' responses on the board. Have students reach consensus on the sequencing of the different activities.

Presentation

3. Invite four volunteers to the front of the room. Give each one an 8-1/2" x 11" picture. Tell the volunteers not to show their pictures to the class. Have the volunteers describe what's happening in their pictures. Using the numbers 1–4 on the board, have the class tell you the order in which each of the students should stand, first, second, third, or fourth, based on the action in their pictures. Ask the volunteers to stand in that order and to reveal their pictures. Have the class decide if the sequence is correct.

Practice

4. Divide the class into groups of six and tell students they will each be getting one picture from a set of six. Point out that they must conceal their pictures from their fellow group members. Explain that students will take turns describing their pictures. Then each student will repeat his description, and the group will decide where that particular picture fits into the sequence 1–6.
5. Distribute the picture sets to each group, one picture per student.
6. Set a 15-minute time limit for students, but increase the time if necessary.
7. Once the time is up, describe one picture at a time in order. See if students challenge or agree with your sequence. Ask for volunteers to describe any other possible sequences.

Follow-up

8. Have the class dictate the party story to you as you write it on the board. Give students time to copy it.

Variations

To make this activity easier, use the activity sheet with the picture cards in sequence to guide students in telling the story.

To make this activity more challenging, have students add to the original picture story or create a different ending.

Welcome to Leola's

Focus: Ordering from a menu, making requests, and working in a restaurant.

Materials: Activity sheet, p. 42; pads and pencils (one each per eight students); paper clips; dining table realia (paper plates, cups, cutlery, napkins); **Family Restaurant and Cocktail Lounge,** and **Restaurant Verbs, Dictionary, pp. 16–17.**

Before class, duplicate a class set of the activity sheet. Set aside half the set to use as restaurant menus. (Do not cut these apart.) Cut apart the pictures on the other half-class set to serve as restaurant food. Clip together sets of each kind of food. Collect the pads, pencils, and realia.

Preview

1. Tell students that they will be eating or working at Leola's family restaurant, of which you are the manager.
2. Direct students to open their dictionaries to pages 16 and 17. Using *Wh*-questions, get students to talk about what's happening on these two pages: "Who's ordering from the menu?" "What's the cook/busboy doing?" Have students tell you about some of the problems that occur in restaurants, such as cold food, burned food, slow service, missing table items, and incorrect orders.
3. Practice taking and giving food orders from a menu, using scratch paper and the activity sheet menu on page 42 as a sample.

Presentation

4. Divide the class in half and assign half the class the role of "restaurant workers" and the other half the role of "customers." Have the customers form groups of four and decide on their family roles (mother, father, child, grandparent). Have the restaurant workers form groups of four and decide on their jobs (cook, busperson, server, cashier/host).
5. Distribute the menus to the restaurant

workers and allow them five minutes to price each menu item. Tell the customers to discuss what they'd each like for lunch. At the end of the time limit, collect the priced menus for later use in the role play.
6. Set up a table in front of the room and write the following steps on the board:
   a. set the table   g. talk to the cook
   b. seat the customers   h. cook
   c. pass out menus   i. serve
   d. read the menus   j. get the check
   e. order   k. clear the table
   f. take the order   l. pay/leave a tip
7. Ask one group of restaurant workers and one group of customers to act out the steps of the role play. Encourage the class to assist the actors over any rough spots. Show the class the cut-up food pictures that the cook uses to fill the customers' orders.
8. Review any special language problems from the demonstration (step 7) <u>before proceeding with the role play.</u>

Practice

9. Define three areas in your classroom: the entrance, the dining room, and the kitchen. Put the cut-up food pictures in the kitchen area and the tableware and priced menus in the dining area. Give each server a pad and pencil. Direct students to the appropriate areas: cooks to the kitchen, cashiers or hosts/hostesses to the entrance, buspeople and servers to the dining room, customers to the door. Have students begin the role play.
10. Circulate as manager, checking the quality of service and listening to complaints. Tell the servers when it's time to give out the checks and to end the role play.

Follow-up

11. Use the experiences from the role play to generate a class discussion on the quality of the restaurant and its employees.

Your Notes

What'll Ya Have? (See Teacher's Notes, page 32.)

- Listen to the people ordering food in a coffee shop.
- Circle the correct items in each order.

1.

Main Dish

(hamburger)	(w/ ketchup)	mustard
hot dog	w/ ketchup	mustard
taco	beef	chicken
pizza	cheese	pepperoni
fried chicken		

Sides

mashed potatoes
(french fries)
(small salad)

Beverages

(cola)	S	M	(L)	
milk	S		L	
tea	w/ lemon			
coffee	w/ cream			

2.

Main Dish

hamburger	w/ ketchup	mustard
hot dog	w/ ketchup	mustard
taco	beef	chicken
pizza	cheese	pepperoni
fried chicken		

Sides

mashed potatoes
french fries
small salad

Beverages

cola	S	M	L	
milk	S		L	
tea	w/ lemon			
coffee	w/ cream			

3.

Main Dish

hamburger	w/ ketchup	mustard
hot dog	w/ ketchup	mustard
taco	beef	chicken
pizza	cheese	pepperoni
fried chicken		

Sides

mashed potatoes
french fries
small salad

Beverages

cola	S	M	L	
milk	S		L	
tea	w/ lemon			
coffee	w/ cream			

4.

Main Dish

hamburger	w/ ketchup	mustard
hot dog	w/ ketchup	mustard
taco	beef	chicken
pizza	cheese	pepperoni
fried chicken		

Sides

mashed potatoes
french fries
small salad

Beverages

cola	S	M	L	
milk	S		L	
tea	w/ lemon			
coffee	w/ cream			

5.

Main Dish

hamburger	w/ ketchup	mustard
hot dog	w/ ketchup	mustard
taco	beef	chicken
pizza	cheese	pepperoni
fried chicken		

Sides

mashed potatoes
french fries
small salad

Beverages

cola	S	M	L	
milk	S		L	
tea	w/ lemon			
coffee	w/ cream			

What's on the Menu? (see Teacher's Notes, page 33.)

- Look at the menu below.
- Take turns asking your partner questions about the missing prices.
- Write in the missing prices.
- Use this conversation as a model:
    How much is a chicken sandwich?
        What kind of sandwich?
    A chicken sandwich.
        Let's see . . . a chicken sandwich is $3.50.

A

Gloria's Kitchen

• Sandwiches •	• Soups • (by the cup)	• Salads •	• Desserts •
Chicken **$3.50**	Tomato - _____ -	Chef's Salad - $5.25 -	Apple Pie - _____ -
Cheese - _____ -	Vegetable - 95¢ -	Green Salad - _____ -	Peach Pie - $1.50 -
Roast Beef - $4.25 -	Turkey - _____ -	Fruit Salad - $1.95 -	Cherry Pie - $2.25 -

--- ✂

- Look at the menu below.
- Take turns asking your partner questions about the missing prices.
- Write in the missing prices.
- Use this conversation as a model:
    How much is a chicken sandwich?
        What kind of sandwich?
    A chicken sandwich.
        Let's see . . . a chicken sandwich is $3.50.

B

Gloria's Kitchen

• Sandwiches •	• Soups • (by the cup)	• Salads •	• Desserts •
Chicken **$3.50**	Tomato - 95¢ -	Chef's Salad - _____ -	Apple Pie - $2.50 -
Cheese - $2.75 -	Vegetable - _____ -	Green Salad - $2.00 -	Peach Pie - _____ -
Roast Beef - _____ -	Turkey - $1.25 -	Fruit Salad - _____ -	Cherry Pie - $2.25 -

Set the Table (See Teacher's Notes, page 34.)

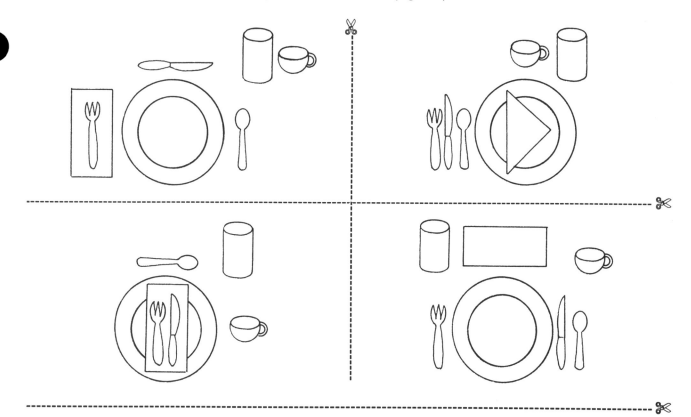

Dining Survey (See Teacher's Notes, page 35.)

- Take turns asking and answering questions about food and restaurants.
- Record your classmate's answers on the grid.

NAME	WHAT'S YOUR FAVORITE KIND OF FOOD?	WHAT'S YOUR FAVORITE DESSERT?	WHAT'S YOUR FAVORITE BEVERAGE?	WHAT'S YOUR FAVORITE RESTAURANT?

- After you complete the grid, discuss these questions with your group:
  - Is there a difference between men's and women's answers?
  - Is there a food, dessert, or beverage that's popular in your group?
  - Is there one restaurant that's popular in your group?

It's a Party (See Teacher's Notes, page 36.)

Welcome to Leola's (See Teacher's Notes, page 37.)

salad | soup | baked potato | baked beans

chicken | spaghetti | steak | pizza

ice cream | jello | pie | cake

cola | lemon-lime soda | coffee | milk

Buying and Describing Clothes
Teacher's Notes and Activity Sheets

Reproducible activity sheets on pages 53–56.

Cold Weather Clothes

> **Focus:** Identifying outdoor clothing.
>
> **Materials:** Answer Cards and Don't Look Mask, p. 179; **Outdoor Clothes, Dictionary, p. 19.**
>
> ───────────────
>
> *Before class, duplicate and cut apart a class set of the Answer Cards and Don't Look Mask. Look over the silent drill questions and the target vocabulary (step 4 below).*

Preview

1. Hold up a set of answer cards and tell students that they will be listening to and answering a series of questions by raising the correct answer card.
2. Direct students to open their dictionaries to page 19. Ask students to identify the people in this scene by their clothing and location in the picture (a man in a yellow windbreaker, a woman on the right). Talk about what the people are doing.

Presentation

3. Distribute the answer cards and masks. Have students cover the vocabulary at the bottom of the page and listen to your questions. Ask the first question: "Is the man in the yellow *windbreaker* wearing a green *backpack?*" Tell your students to raise the Yes card if the answer is yes, the No card if it is no, and the Not Sure card when there's not enough information to answer yes or no. Get class consensus on the first answer before continuing.

Practice (with Answers)

4. Ask the following questions:
   Is the man in the yellow *windbreaker* wearing a green *backpack?* (Yes)
   Is the the girl with the *ice skates* wearing *blue jeans?* (No)
   Are both men in the picture wearing *gloves* and *caps?* (Yes)
   Is the man in the blue *jacket* wearing a *flannel shirt?* (No)
   Is the woman on the far left wearing a *crewneck sweater* and a heavy pink *parka?* (Yes)
   Is the girl with the white *earmuffs* and *down vest* wearing a *V-neck sweater?* (No)
   Is the woman in the pink *beret* wearing a *coat?* (Yes)
   Are the man and woman on the left wearing *hiking boots* and *blue jeans?* (Yes)
   Is the woman with the dark *hat* and red *scarf* wearing *tights?* (Not sure)
   Is every person in the picture wearing *gloves* or *mittens?* (Yes)

Follow-up

5. Have students, in pairs, make up two additional Yes/No/Not Sure questions and take turns asking the class their questions. The class responds using the answer cards.

The Bus Stop

Focus: Identifying people by their clothing.

Materials: Don't Look Mask, p. 179; listening cassette; **Everyday Clothes, Dictionary, pp. 20–21.**

Before class, duplicate and cut apart a class set of the Don't Look Mask. Look over the target vocabulary in the tapescript below.

Preview

1. Tell students that they will be listening to a bus driver describe people by the clothes they're wearing.
2. Direct students to open their dictionaries to pages 20 and 21. Looking at the pages, have students, in small groups, list five things they would wear for work and five things they would wear for recreation. Ask volunteers from each group to read their lists. Add any missing target vocabulary.

Presentation

3. Distribute the masks and have students cover the vocabulary at the bottom of the pages. Tell students to listen to the tape and to point to the correct pictures in their dictionaries. Assure students that they will have several opportunities to hear the listening passage.
4. Play the tape through "I wonder what he's reading about?" Stop the tape and check to be sure that students are pointing to the man in the uniform on the far right (page 21). Replay this section of the tape until all students are pointing to the correct person.

Practice

5. Play the tape, stopping when necessary. Replay the tape two to five times.

Follow-up

6. Check for comprehension of the target vocabulary by asking questions, such as "Where is the shopping bag?" Students can respond by saying "#18" or by pointing to the correct picture.

Variation

To make this activity more challenging, have students, in pairs, make up cues about the people at the bus stop, present them, and have the rest of the class guess which person the cues describe.

Tapescript (with Answers)

Listen to bus driver, Martin Shift, describe people at the bus stop. Point to the people you hear Martin talking about.

Oh, there's Mr. Trenton. He's wearing his *uniform (45)*, that means he's going to work. He's the one wearing *glasses (44)* and reading the *newspaper (48)*. I wonder what he's reading about.* And of course, Ms. Ryder is looking at her watch. She always thinks I'm late. That's a nice pink suit she's wearing. Last week she left her *briefcase (37)* on the bus. Hmm . . . Mrs. Brown is carrying an *umbrella (24)*. It matches her blue dress, but the *umbrella (24)* makes me nervous. I hate to drive in the rain.* I can see that Mrs. Miller was at the shopping mall. She's wearing green *sandals (19)* to go with her green skirt. What does she have in that *shopping bag (18)*? It looks so heavy.* I see Craig's ready for his construction job. He's wearing his *hard hat (28)* and blue *overalls (30)*. He's working on that new building downtown.* Do you see Gary Benton? He's the man running in the red *tank top (13)* and *shorts (14)*. He's running in the marathon next week. I wonder if he wants to race the bus . . . Nahhh. He's too fast for me! (heh, heh)* I see Donna's all ready for school; she's wearing a yellow *cardigan (26)* and *pants (27)*. Looks like that book bag she's carrying is really full.* Oh, wow! Neil Edwards certainly looks good in his blue *blazer (2)* and gray *slacks (4)*. Oh, yes. He's going for a job interview today.* Oh, no! Not again! Barbara's looking in her *wallet (9)* for a dollar bill. That means she doesn't have change for the bus. I bet she doesn't have any spare change either because she's wearing a *sweatshirt (8)* and *sweatpants (10)* with [groan] no pockets.* Well, it's time to pick them all up. Hey, who's that guy? The one wearing the gray *suit (40)* with a *vest (39)* and carrying his *raincoat (38)*! Oh great! My supervisor's going to ride the bus with me. It must be his day off. I wish it were my day off too!

A Phone Call Home

> **Focus:** Categorizing items of clothing.
>
> **Materials:** Activity Sheet, p. 53; listening cassette; **Outdoor Clothes, Underwear and Sleepwear,** and **Jewelry and Cosmetics, Dictionary, pp. 19, 22, and 23.**
>
> ___
>
> *Before class, duplicate a class set of the activity sheet. Look over the target vocabulary in the tapescript below.*

Preview

1. Tell students that they will be listening to a woman calling home because she and her husband forgot to pack some clothes for a trip.
2. Direct students to open their dictionaries to pages 19, 22, and 23. Ask students to tell you which outdoor clothing, underwear, sleepwear, jewelry, and cosmetics they would take on a trip. Point out any important items students forget to mention, being sure to include any missing target vocabulary.

Presentation

3. Copy the three clothing categories and the example (√) from the activity sheet onto the board. Explain the task to the students, and assure them that they will have several opportunities to hear the listening passage.
4. Have students listen to the tape through "I'm sure they're on the hamper," and review the example on the board.
5. Distribute the activity sheets and review the directions.

Practice

6. Play the tape, stopping when necessary.
7. Take a survey of the number of checks made under each category. Get class consensus on the accuracy of the numbers. If class response is inaccurate, have students repeat the activity using the second set of categories (B). If necessary, replay the tape a third time using the third set of categories (C).

8. Invite a volunteer to do the activity on the board as you play the tape one last time.

Follow-up

9. Have students, in pairs, list the clothing items they remember from the tape. Then have pairs combine to compare lists.

___

Tapescript (with Answers)

Listen to Sofia talking about the clothing she forgot to pack. Make a check in the correct box.

Hello, mother? Yes, we've arrived and we're fine. Are the children being good for you? I hope so. Listen, Mom, Jack and I forgot to pack some things and we wondered if you could send them to us right away . . . You can? Great! Please send Jack's green *pajamas*. He can't sleep without them. I'm sure they're on the hamper.* And he forgot his *slippers* too. They're under the bed, I think. We can't walk barefoot around here.* It's so cold, Jack says he needs his heavy *jacket*. That's downstairs in the hall closet.* Can you believe I forgot all my new *pantyhose*? They're probably hanging over the bathtub. I can't go anywhere without my hose.* While you're in the bathroom, can you look for my *makeup*? It's important to look glamorous here.* Oh, and look on the dresser for Jack's gold *cuff links*. Yes, the ones you gave him for his birthday.* You'll have to go out to the garage because Jack left his brown *gloves* in the car. His hands get so cold without them.* Please look for my black *slip*. I need to wear everything I can under my clothes! . . . No, I have no idea where I left it.* You know what else, Mother? Even my neck gets cold here. I left my *scarf* on the table in the hall.* And you should find my *ski cap* right next to it, too. We're going skiing next week.* Wait a minute, Mother. Jack is telling me something. Right . . . could you look for his black *hiking boots*? I know they're too big for his feet, but he likes them. They're somewhere in the garage.* He can wear my wool *knee socks* with them, but of course we forgot those too. They're in the laundry room.* They say it's going to snow so you'd better send my blue winter *coat*. It's either in the downstairs hall closet or it's at the cleaner's. OK, Mom, I think that's all we need. That won't be too much trouble for you, will it, Mother? . . . Mother? . . . Mother? Hello? Operator, I've been cut off!

(**Answers:** Outdoor Clothing—6 checks; Underwear & Sleepwear—5 checks; Jewelry & Cosmetics—3 checks)

Clothes Closet

> **Focus:** Identifying men's or women's clothing.
> Note* This activity creates the clothing inventory for the ABC Department Store Activity, p. 50.
>
> **Materials:** Clothing Picture Cards, #21–#40, p. 181; listening cassette; light and dark color crayons or markers (1 of each per student); scissors (1 pair per 4 students); 20 large envelopes; **Everyday Clothes, Describing Clothes,** and **Appendix, Dictionary, pp. 20–21, 24, and 104.**
>
> *Before class, duplicate a class set of the picture card page but do not cut the picture cards apart. Write the following categories on the board: Women's Clothing, Men's Clothing, and Unisex Clothing.*

Preview

1. Tell students that they will be listening for descriptions of different men's or women's clothing, and coloring in pictures of these clothes.
2. Direct students to look at page 24 in their dictionaries. Review the vocabulary depicted by items 9, 10, and 17–22, by having students identify what their classmates are wearing: "Pablo's wearing a *dark plaid* shirt."
3. Ask students to name three different articles of clothing: one worn by a man, one by a woman, and one that can be worn by either. Draw the clothing items on the board under the appropriate category. Invite volunteers to pattern the clothing according to their classmates' directions: "Make the skirt *striped.*"

Presentation

4. Distribute the picture cards and the crayons or markers. Play the tape through number 1, "Make it *striped.*" Stop the tape. Ask students on which article of clothing they will put stripes. Point out that students' answers may be different and still be correct. Review directions and assure students that they will have several opportunities to hear the listening passage.

Practice

6. Play the tape, stopping after each item. When necessary, replay each item two to five times.
7. Have students, in pairs, share their completed picture pages. Elicit students' responses by calling out a pattern and having students tell you which of their clothing items has that pattern.

Follow-up

8. Have student pairs take turns telling each other how to pattern or color the remaining clothing items on their picture pages.
9. Distribute the scissors. Have students cut apart their clothing pictures. Then review the vocabulary by collecting the pictures item by item (all the ties, dresses, shoes).

*Save each group of items in labeled envelopes to use as the clothing inventory for the ABC Department Store role play.

Tapescript

Listen to the directions. Design or color in the clothing.
1. Find something a man wears with shoes. Make them a *solid light color.*
2. Find something a woman wears. Make it a *solid light* color.
3. Find something either a man or woman can wear. Make it *checked.*
4. Find something a man wears. Make it *striped.*
5. Find something a woman wears on her feet. Make them a *solid dark* color.
6. Find something either a man or woman can wear. Put a *print* on it.
7. Find something a man wears. Make it a *solid dark* color.
8. Find something either a woman or man can wear. Make it *plaid.*
9. Find something a woman wears. Make *dark polka dots* on it.
10. Find something either a woman or man can wear. Make it *striped.*

Skirts and Shirts

> **Focus:** Asking for and giving clothing prices.
>
> **Materials:** Activity sheet, p. 54; manila folders (one per pair); a full-page newspaper photo ad featuring clothing; **Underwear and Sleepwear, Dictionary, p. 22.**
>
> *Before class, duplicate half a class set of the activity sheet. Cut apart the A and B sections of the sheets and keep them separate. Copy the conversation from the activity sheet onto the board.*

Preview

1. Tell students that they will be working in pairs to find out the prices of clothing items in a newspaper ad.
2. Show students the newspaper clothing ad. Ask students about the items, prices, and patterns, if any, featured in the ad. Write a few of the items mentioned, with their prices, on the board. As you write, clarify the prices by asking questions, such as "$15 or $50?"

Presentation

3. Use the conversation on the board to model the language and clarification strategy you want students to use in the activity. Have the class practice the conversation, substituting different clothing items from the ad.
4. Pair students and assign each one an A or a B role. Explain to students that they will each have ads with different prices missing. Point out that the missing information is in their partner's ad. Tell students that they will take turns asking for and giving the missing prices in order to complete their ads.
5. Distribute a manila folder to each pair, to be propped up between the students as a screen. Distribute the A and B activity sheets to the appropriate partners. Instruct students to look only at their own papers and not at their partner's.
6. Tell students to look at the example on their ads and tell you the price of a striped shirt. Check comprehension by asking A students, "How much is the solid white skirt?" Ask B students, "How much is the solid black shirt?"
7. Have one pair demonstrate the activity by asking for and giving prices from their ads. Remind students to look only at their own ads.

Practice

8. Have students, in pairs, ask and answer questions about the missing prices in their ads. Once they complete the task, partners can compare ads to be sure they are the same.

Follow-up

9. Have pairs form groups of four. Direct the groups to look at page 22 in their dictionaries and to create a newspaper ad featuring the sleepwear on the dictionary page. Encourage the students to draw various patterns on the clothing. Groups can post their ads around the room and discuss the best prices on pajamas, slippers, and so on.

Clothing Go Around

Focus: Demonstrating knowledge about clothing.

Materials: Activity sheet, p. 55; Picture Cards, #21–#40, p. 181; coins; scratch paper; four 8-1/2" x 11" sheets of blank paper; clips or small envelopes; **Outdoor Clothes, Everyday Clothes, Underwear and Sleepwear, Jewelry and Cosmetics,** and **Describing Clothes, Dictionary, pp. 19–24.**

Before class, duplicate the activity sheet (one per four students). Duplicate the picture cards (one set per four students). Cut apart the picture cards and clip or put them together in small envelopes. Draw the following pictures on the 8-1/2" x 11" sheets of paper (one picture per sheet): a short sleeved shirt, a skirt, a tie, and a blouse.

Preview

1. Tell students that they are going to test their knowledge of clothing by playing a board game with their classmates.
2. Direct students to open their dictionaries to page 19. Write the following statements and questions on the board: "Say it and spell it," "Do you have this item in your closet?" and "How much does it cost?" Ask the class to choose one clothing item from page 19 and to respond to each statement or question on the board. For additional practice, repeat the procedure using dictionary pages 20–24.

Presentation

3. Copy the activity sheet onto the board, filling in only the first four squares. Place the 8-1/2" x 11" clothing pictures on the chalk ledge, face down. Invite three volunteers to the front of the room. Have the volunteers write their names on separate pieces of scratch paper, while you do the same. Tape the papers to the "Start" square. Explain that the papers are the game markers.

4. Show the class a coin and demonstrate flipping it "heads" and "tails." Flip the coin and move your marker on the board, one space for heads, two spaces for tails. Move your marker to the square "Pick a card: Say it and spell it" or "Name something a woman wears." Have the class read the directions aloud. Follow the directions. Play two rounds of the game with the three volunteers. Get class consensus on the accuracy of the volunteers' responses. Point out that when a response is not correct, the player cannot flip the coin on her next turn and must answer the same question again.

Practice

5. Divide the class into groups of four. Distribute the activity sheets (game boards), picture card sets, coins, and scratch paper to each group. Have each group create four "markers" and place them on the "Start" square.
6. Check for general understanding of the game by asking yes/no questions, such as "Do I move two spaces for heads?" and "Do I pick a card from the top of the pile?"
7. Set a 20-minute time limit for the game and begin play.
8. Circulate and monitor student practice. (In cases where groups cannot come to consensus, you serve as referee.)

Follow-up

9. Divide the class into two teams, A and B. Copy the activity sheet onto the board, replacing the directions with numbers. Have team members take turns flipping coins and answering your questions (the original questions or new ones).

Variation

Divide the class into groups of five. Students 1 and 2 form team A, students 3 and 4 form team B, and student 5 serves as the referee. Proceed as before (step 9). Allow referees to use the dictionary and other resources to decide if spelling and other responses are accurate.

ABC Department Store

Focus: Asking and answering questions about clothing sizes, prices, colors, and patterns.

Materials: Activity sheet, p. 53; colored-in picture cards from "Clothes Closet" activity, p. 47; seven sheets of 8-1/2" x 11" paper; small slips of scratch paper; a large envelope; colored markers, **Describing Clothes, Dictionary, p. 24.**

Before class, duplicate half a class set of the activity sheet. Arrange the picture cards from "Clothes Closet" (p. 47) into these departments: Men's Clothing, Women's Clothing, Accessories. (Use the activity sheet as a guide.) Make an 8-1/2" x 11" sign for each department. Draw an outline of a tie on each of the remaining four 8-1/2" x 11" sheets.

Preview

1. Tell students that they will be buying or selling clothing in the ABC Department Store, of which you are the manager.
2. Direct students to open their dictionaries to page 24. Show the four 8-1/2" x 11" pictures of ties. Have students tell you how to pattern or color each tie. Practice asking for and giving the price of each tie. Write the prices on the back of the pictures.
3. Post the three department signs on the board and ask students for examples of clothing items from each department. Discuss sizes and colors.

Presentation

4. Divide the class in half. Assign one half the role of "salespeople" and the other half the role of "customers." Have the customers form pairs and the salespeople form three groups (to represent each department) of four to six students.
5. Have each student who is a salesperson write his name on a slip of paper and put it in the

large envelope. Have each customer pick a name from the envelope. Distribute the activity sheets to the customers. Have customers, in pairs, take 10 minutes to decide on three things they want to buy for the classmates whose names they have picked.
6. Assign each group of salespeople one of the three departments (Men's Clothing, Women's Clothing, Accessories). Distribute a related and appropriate set of clothing pictures to each salesperson in the group (for example, in Men's Clothing, student 1 gets the set of pants, student 2 gets the set of shirts, and so on). While the customers do step 5, have the salespeople price their inventories and write the prices on the back of the pictures.
7. Write these steps on the board:
   a. offer to help
   b. identify the item you want
   c. give the price
   d. ask to see more items
   e. show different items
   f. give the prices
   g. buy an item
   h. continue to shop
   Place the tie pictures on the chalk ledge and invite one salesperson and one customer to act out a purchase following the steps of the role play. Encourage the class to assist the actors over any rough spots.
8. Review any special language problems from the demonstration (step 7) <u>before proceeding with the role play</u>.

Practice

9. Post the department signs around the room and direct the salespeople to set up their clothing inventory in the correct area. Have students begin the role play. When a sale is made, have the customer take the picture card.
10. Circulate as manager, checking the quality of service. Suggest to salespeople when it is time to end the role play.

Follow-up

11. Discuss what people say when they give or receive gifts. Have customers distribute the gifts they purchased for their classmates.

Fashion Show

Preview

1. Tell students that they will be working in small groups to design, draw, and write about the clothes for a model.
2. Direct students to open their dictionaries to pages 19–23. Ask students to name all the clothing items a woman can wear at one time. List these items on the board and have students identify which ones the fashion models in the posted photos are wearing.

Presentation

3. Tape one of the butcher paper models onto the board. One at a time, draw the items of clothing elicited in step 2 on this model. Ask the class to tell you how to color and pattern each item. Once the model's outfit is finished, describe it to the class.

Practice

4. Divide students into groups of three, and have them number off 1–3. Distribute an activity sheet to each group, along with the markers.
5. Tell students they will have 10 minutes to "dress" their model. Have student 1 draw and color in one item of clothing on the model and then pass the sheet to student 2. Student 2 draws and then passes the sheet to student 3. Students continue "dressing" their model, passing the sheet around the group until you call time.
6. After 10 minutes, have each group write up a short description of their model's outfit on the activity sheet. The group then chooses a narrator to read their description to the class. Refer students to dictionary pages 19–24 for vocabulary. Set a 20-minute time limit to complete this step.
7. Tape each group's model onto the board and have group narrators take turns presenting their model.

Follow-up

8. At the front of the room, tape the second butcher paper model. Have one person from each group come up and draw something on this composite model. When this model is dressed, elicit a description of her outfit from the class, writing the description on the board exactly as the students tell it to you. Have students read the description aloud and copy it.

The following is a typical level-one story: This is Sofia Gravitz. She wearing a red dress with a black belt. Her stocking are black and her shoes are silver. She's wearing large earrings and necklace. The clothes are beautiful and expensive.

Your Notes

A Phone Call Home (See Teacher's Notes, page 46.)

- Listen to Sofia talking about the clothing she forgot to pack.
- Make a check (√) in the correct box.

A	OUTDOOR CLOTHES	UNDERWEAR AND SLEEPWEAR ✔	JEWELRY AND COSMETICS

B	OUTDOOR CLOTHES	UNDERWEAR AND SLEEPWEAR	JEWELRY AND COSMETICS

C	OUTDOOR CLOTHES	UNDERWEAR AND SLEEPWEAR	JEWELRY AND COSMETICS

--- ✂

ABC Department Store (See Teacher's Notes, page 50.)

- Decide what you're going to buy for your classmate.
- Write the color and pattern on the line in front of the items.

SHOPPING LIST

Men's clothing
_____ sweater
_____ tie
_____ socks
_____ shoes
_____ jacket
_____ jeans
_____ T-shirt
_____ coat
_____ shirt
_____ pajamas
_____ suit

Women's clothing
_____ sweater
_____ dress
_____ socks
_____ jacket
_____ jeans
_____ T-shirt
_____ coat
_____ blouse
_____ pajamas

Accessories
_____ watch
_____ chain
_____ purse
_____ gloves
_____ ring
_____ belt

Skirts and Shirts (see Teacher's Notes, page 48.)

- Look at the clothing ad below.
- Take turns asking your partner questions about the missing prices.
- Write in the missing prices.
- Use this conversation as a model:
    How much is a plaid shirt?
        $13.00.
    $13.00 or $30.00?
        $13.00.

A

✂

- Look at the clothing ad below.
- Take turns asking your partner questions about the missing prices.
- Write in the missing prices.
- Use this conversation as a model:
    How much is a plaid shirt?
        $13.00.
    $13.00 or $30.00?
        $13.00.

B

Clothing Go Around (See Teacher's Notes, page 49.)

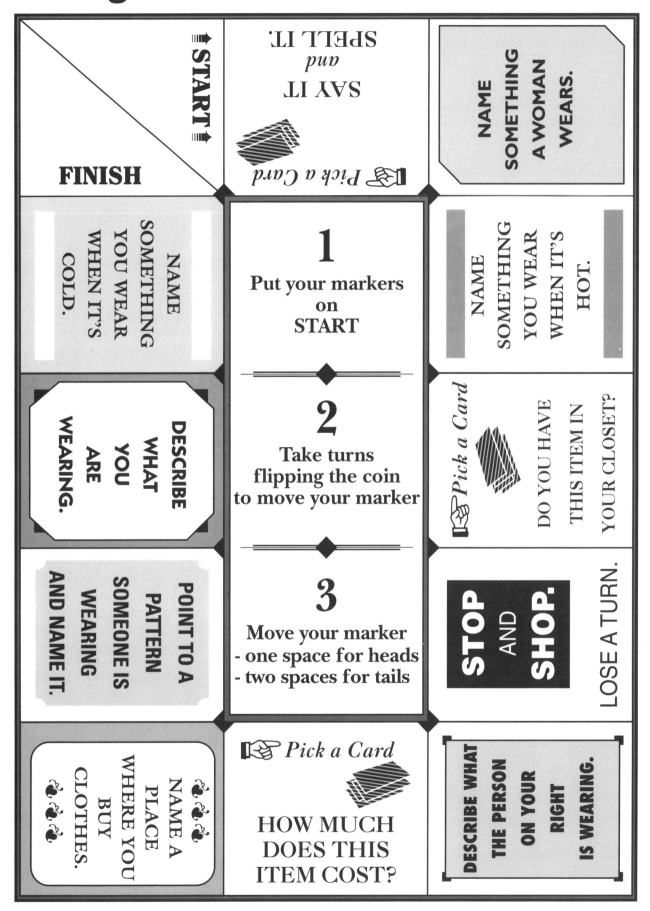

START →

SAY IT and SPELL IT.

☞ Pick a Card

NAME SOMETHING A WOMAN WEARS.

FINISH

NAME SOMETHING YOU WEAR WHEN IT'S COLD.

1
Put your markers on START

NAME SOMETHING YOU WEAR WHEN IT'S HOT.

DESCRIBE WHAT YOU ARE WEARING.

2
Take turns flipping the coin to move your marker

☞ Pick a Card

DO YOU HAVE THIS ITEM IN YOUR CLOSET?

POINT TO A PATTERN SOMEONE IS WEARING AND NAME IT.

3
Move your marker
- one space for heads
- two spaces for tails

STOP AND **SHOP.**

LOSE A TURN.

NAME A PLACE WHERE YOU BUY CLOTHES.

☞ Pick a Card

HOW MUCH DOES THIS ITEM COST?

DESCRIBE WHAT THE PERSON ON YOUR RIGHT IS WEARING.

Fashion Show (See Teacher's Notes, page 51.)

- Take turns drawing clothes on this model.
- Include shoes, jewelry, and other accessories.

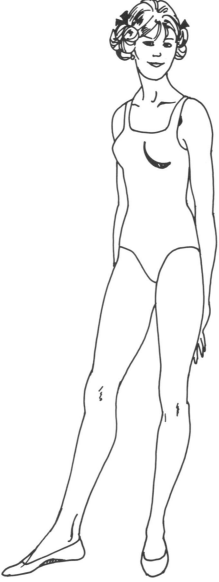

- Work together to write a description of your model's outfit.

_____

_____

_____

_____

_____

Describing Your Home
Teacher's Notes and Activity Sheets

Activity Title	■ Activity Type	Page
No Place Like Home Students look at a living room in the Dictionary and respond to a series of yes/no questions.	■ Silent Drill	**58**
Company for Dinner Students listen to a woman preparing for a dinner party and point to the correct pictures in the Dictionary.	■ Listen and Point	**59**
Is There Cable TV? Students listen to a realtor talking about various homes and check the correct features of each.	■ Listening Grid	**60**
Where's the Teakettle? Students look at identical pictures of a kitchen and ask for and give the location of various kitchen items.	■ Information Gap	**61**
Where Does the Sofa Go? Tenants direct student movers to place furniture in an apartment.	■ TPR Pairs	**62**
Lost and Found Students try to locate a missing watch by asking yes/no questions.	■ Interactive Drill	**63**
Garage Sale Students price and negotiate the sale of various items in a garage sale setting.	■ Role Play	**64**
Design a Room Students design different rooms in a house and write a description of the home they've created.	■ Language Experience	**65**

Reproducible activity sheets on pages 67–70.

No Place Like Home

Focus: Identifying items in a living room.

Materials: Answer Cards and Don't Look Mask, p. 179; **The Living Room, Dictionary, p. 28.**

Before class, duplicate and cut apart a class set of the Answer Cards and Don't Look Mask. Look over the silent drill questions and the target vocabulary (step 4 below).

Preview

1. Hold up a set of answer cards and tell students that they will be listening to and answering a series of questions by raising the correct answer card.
2. Direct students to open their dictionaries to page 28. Ask students to identify the items in the living room, such as television, bookcase, carpet, sofa.

Presentation

3. Distribute the answer cards and masks. Have students cover the vocabulary at the bottom of the page and listen to your questions about the pictures. Ask the first question: "Is there a *lamp* on the *coffee table?*" Tell students to raise the Yes card if the answer is yes, the No card if it is no, and the Not Sure card when there's not enough information to answer yes or no. Get class consensus on the first answer before continuing.

Practice (with Answers)

4. Ask the following questions:
   Is there a *lamp* on the *coffee table?* (No)
   Is there a *painting* on the *wall?* (Yes)
   Is there a *book* under the *desk?* (Not sure)
   Is there a *television* in the *wall unit?* (Yes)
   Is there a *coffee table* in front of the *fireplace?* (No)
   Is there a man sitting on the *sofa?* (No)
   Is there a *stereo* in the *bookcase?* (No)
   Are there *drapes* on the *window?* (Yes)
   Is there *wall-to-wall carpeting* on the *floor?* (Yes)
   Is there a *fire* in the *fireplace?* (Yes)

Follow-up

5. Discuss where students would shop for some of the items in the picture. Talk about which stores have the best prices. Ask students to tell where the stores are located.

Company for Dinner

Focus: Identifying items in a dining room.

Materials: Don't Look Mask, p. 179; listening cassette; place settings including a plate, glass, cup, napkin, fork, knife, and spoon (one per four students); **The Dining Room, Dictionary, p. 29.**

Before class, duplicate a class set of the Don't Look Mask. Look over the target vocabulary in the tapescript below.

Preview

1. Tell students that they will be listening to a woman describe her dining room as she makes last-minute party preparations.
2. Direct students to open their dictionaries to page 29. Write the following categories of household items on the board: furniture, utensils, dishes, and containers. Ask the class to identify several items for each category. Write students' suggestions on the board and add any target vocabulary that is missing.

Presentation

3. Distribute the masks and have students cover the vocabulary at the bottom of the page. Tell students to listen to the tape and to point to the correct pictures in their dictionaries. Assure students that they will have several opportunities to hear the listening passage.
4. Play the tape through "My brother may bring his girlfriend." Stop the tape and check to be sure that students are pointing to picture #17. Replay this section of the tape until all students are pointing to picture #17.

Practice

5. Play the tape, stopping when necessary. Replay the tape two to five times.

Follow-up

6. Check for comprehension of the target vocabulary by asking the class to imagine that they're preparing for a party. Ask questions, such as "Where's the coffeepot?" Students can respond by saying the number or pointing to the correct picture.

Variation

To make the follow-up more challenging, divide the class into groups of four. Distribute a place setting to each group and have them "set a table." Have one person in each group step outside, while the group removes one item from the place setting. Call the students back and have them try to remember what's missing. Repeat the activity three times, giving each group member an opportunity to go outside.

Tapescript (with Answers)

Listen to Nancy preparing for a dinner party. Point to the items you hear Nancy talking about.

Hurry, Steve. Everyone will be here in just a few minutes! Do you think we need to get another *chair (17)*? My brother may bring his girlfriend.* Maybe it's a little early to light the *candles (27)*, but they look so pretty.* Did you remember to polish the *buffet (29)*? Well, it's too late now!* We should move the *coffeepot (18)* into the kitchen. It's too early to serve coffee.* The *cups (20)* and *saucers (21)* are too crowded. Let's move them too.* Steve, be careful with that *pitcher (4)* you're holding! That was an anniversary gift from my parents, remember?* Don't pour any water in the *wine glass (5)*. That's the small one on the table.* And watch your head—you almost hit it on the *chandelier (3)*!* Steve, do you like these *napkins (14)*? They're much nicer than the paper ones we usually use.* Maybe I should take them off the *plates (13)*. No, I think they look nice.* I'll put the *fork (12)* on the left side. Or maybe on the right?* This *spoon (8)* I'm holding is dirty. Would you get another one?* And don't forget to close the doors on the *china closet (2)*. I want everything to be perfect for our company.* Oh no, there's a spot on this *tablecloth (16)*! We'll have to set the *table (7)* all over again! [sound of a doorbell]

Is There Cable TV?

> **Focus:** Identifying different features in a home.
>
> **Materials:** Activity sheet, p. 67; Don't Look Mask, p. 179; listening cassette; **Houses, The Dining Room, The Kitchen, The Bedroom,** and **The Baby's Room, Dictionary, pp. 27, 29–30, and 32–33.**
> _____
> *Before class, duplicate a class set of the activity sheet and the Don't Look Mask. Look over the target vocabulary in the tapescript below and on the activity sheet.*

Preview

1. Tell students that they will be listening to a realtor describe different homes.
2. Direct students to open their dictionaries to pages 29–30 and 32–33, and to review the headings for each page. Have students close their dictionaries and brainstorm the names of the different rooms and special features they would expect to find in a house or an apartment. List the rooms and features on the board.
3. Direct students to open their dictionaries to page 27. Distribute the Don't Look Masks, and have students cover the vocabulary at the bottom of the page. Have students look at the ranch house (A) and the colonial-style house (B). Ask students, "Is there a . . . ?" for each house, using the different features on the board to complete the questions. When students correctly identify a feature, make a check (√) next to it on the board.

Presentation

4. Copy the list of features and number one (the example) from the activity sheet onto the board. Explain the task to students, and assure them that they will have several opportunities to hear the listening passage.
5. Play the tape through number 1, ". . . you don't really need one." and review the example on the board.

6. Distribute the activity sheets and review the directions.

Practice

7. Play the tape, stopping after each item. When necessary, replay each item two to five times.
8. Elicit students' responses for each item and get class consensus on the accuracy of the answers. Replay the tape to clarify problems.

Follow-up

9. Have students, in pairs, ask each other a series of "Is there a . . . in your home?" questions, using the grid as a cue sheet. Then conduct a class survey of students with fireplaces, dishwashers, large kitchens, and so on.

_____

Tapescript (with Answers)

Listen to Mrs. Diego talking about different homes. Make a check (√) next to the features of each home.

1. Oh, you're going to love this home. It's so cozy and comfortable. There's a *fireplace*—great for romance. [pause] No, there's no *dining room*, but you don't really need one. (*fireplace*)
2. Oh, I'm so excited about this place for you! There's a wonderful large *kitchen*, with the loveliest old stove. And you will just love the *baby's room*. It's bright the way a baby's room should be! [pause] Twins? Congratulations! It's a good thing there's a big *dishwasher*! (*kitchen, baby's room, dishwasher*)
3. This is perfect for your big family! There's a *dining room*, a large *kitchen* and a family room with *cable TV*. [pause] No, there's no *air conditioner*, but summer isn't so bad here. [pause] No, no *dishwasher* either, sorry. [pause] Yes, there's a small *baby's room*. (*dining room, kitchen, cable TV, baby's room*)
4. Guess what! I've found you and your wife an apartment! Yes, it has everything you two want—almost. Uh, there's no *fireplace*. Hard to find in an apartment. [pause] No, there's no *dining room*, but there is a large *kitchen*. [pause] Yes, of course there's a *dishwasher*. And an excellent *air conditioner* too! You'll love this place! (*kitchen, dishwasher, air conditioner*)
5. Mrs. Chong, I have the perfect house! It's a charming ranch house with a large sunny *kitchen* and a beautiful *dining room*. No, no *dishwasher*, but I'm sure you can put one in. Yes, there is a lovely *fireplace*. [pause] A room for a baby? No. [pause] There's no *cable TV* either, but call the cable TV people. I'm sure they'll put it in. (*kitchen, dining room, fireplace*)

Where's the Teakettle?

Focus: Asking for and giving location of kitchen items.

Materials: Activity sheet, p. 68; manila folders (one per pair); **The Kitchen,** and **Prepositions of Description, Dictionary, pp. 30 and 102.**

Before class, duplicate half a class set of the activity sheet. Cut apart the A and B sections of the sheets and keep them separate. Copy the conversation from the activity sheet onto the board.

Preview

1. Tell students that they will be working in pairs to locate items in a kitchen.
2. Direct students to open their dictionaries to page 30. Review the vocabulary by asking students to identify the location of several kitchen items you name. (Students may refer to page 102 for prepositions.)

Presentation

3. Use the conversation on the board to model the language and clarification strategy you want students to use in the activity. Have the class practice the conversation, substituting different kitchen items.
4. Pair students and assign each one an A or a B role. Explain to students that they will each have a kitchen picture with some items missing. Point out that the missing information is in their partner's picture. Tell students that they will take turns asking for and giving this missing information so that they can finish labeling their pictures.
5. Distribute a manila folder to each pair, to be propped up between the students as a screen. Distribute the A and B activity sheets to the appropriate partners. Review the directions and instruct students to look only at their own papers and not at their partner's.

6. Tell students to look at the example and tell you the location of the blender. Check comprehension by asking A students, "Where's the dish towel?" Ask B students, "Where's the cutting board?"
7. Have one pair demonstrate the activity by asking for and giving the location of one kitchen item. Remind students to look only at their own pictures.

Practice

8. Have students, in pairs, ask and answer questions about the missing kitchen items. Once they complete the task, partners can compare pictures to be sure they are the same.

Follow-up

9. Have students make a list of the items in their own kitchens. Then have students, in pairs, compare lists and tell each other where each item is located. Model expressions, such as "I don't have a blender," and "There's no dishwasher."

Where Does the Sofa Go?

Focus: Giving and following directions for arranging furniture.

Materials: Activity sheet, p. 69; five 8-1/2" x 11" blank sheets of paper; tape; manila folders (one per pair); paper clips or small envelopes; **The Living Room, Dictionary, p. 28.**

Before class, duplicate half a class set of the activity sheet. Cut apart living room floor plans #1–#4 and keep them separate. Cut apart the sets of furniture pictures under #5 and keep these sets separate with paper clips or in envelopes. Collect half a class set of manila folders. Draw the following pictures on three of the blank sheets of paper (one item per sheet): a sofa, a lamp, and an easy chair. Copy floor plan #5 onto the board, making it large enough to accommodate the 8-1/2" x 11" drawings. Draw an enlarged version of floor plan #1 on the two remaining sheets of paper.

Preview

1. Tell students that they will be arranging furniture in an apartment according to their partner's directions.
2. Direct students to open their dictionaries to page 28. Discuss the location of the furniture in the room: "Where's the sofa?" "It's in front of the window."
3. Have students tell you where to place the 8-1/2" x 11" sofa, chair, and lamp on the floor plan copied onto the board. As students direct you ("Put the sofa under the window"), carry out their directions by taping the pictures to the board. Incorporate appropriate clarification questions as you respond to the directions, such as "Where?" or "In the center of the room or under the window?"
4. Invite a volunteer to the board to place the same pictures according to your directions. Modify the arrangement from the one used in step 3.

Presentation

5. Ask two of your more advanced students to come to the board. Call one student the "tenant" and the other the "mover." Give the mover the 8-1/2" x 11" "furniture" and the tenant one of the 8-1/2" x 11" copies of floor plan #1. Have the tenant use his picture to tell the mover where to place the furniture on the floor plan on the board. Show the class the other 8-1/2" x 11" floor plan so that the students know what the tenant is looking at. Encourage the class to help the mover and tenant complete their tasks.

Practice

6. Pair students and identify one as tenant, the other as mover. Distribute a manila folder to each pair, to be propped up between the students as a screen. Explain that the tenants will give directions and the movers will place the "furniture" according to those directions.
7. Distribute floor plan #1 to the tenants and floor plan #5 and the "furniture" to the movers. While pairs work on floor plan #1, circulate and monitor their progress. When partners have completed the first floor plan, they can compare pictures and talk about any discrepancies.
8. After pairs finish comparing floor plan #1, have them pick up floor plan #2 and repeat the activity. When partners finish #2, ask them to compare pictures, switch roles, pick up floor plans #3 and #4, and exchange #5 and the "furniture."

Follow-up

9. Divide the class into four teams. Give the first person on each team a blank sheet of paper. Call out the first direction: "Draw a sofa." Have the first person draw the sofa and pass the paper to the next person on the team. Continue giving directions until all team members have had a turn. Have the last student on each team show the team's drawing. Compare drawings and repeat the activity.

Lost and Found

Focus: Locating missing objects by asking yes/no questions.

Materials: Activity sheet, p. 70; Don't Look Mask, p. 179; three 8-1/2" x 11" blank sheets of paper; paper clips; **The Living Room, The Bedroom, The Bathroom,** and **Prepositions of Description, Dictionary, pp. 28, 32, 34, and 102.**

Before class, duplicate and cut apart a class set of the Don't Look Mask. Duplicate one-third of a class set of the activity sheet. Cut apart and clip the cue slips into sets. Copy the following phrases onto the three 8-1/2" x 11" sheets of paper: "I lost my watch in the living room. (It's behind the recliner.)"; "I lost my watch in the bedroom. (It's under the night table.)"; and "I lost my watch in the bathroom. (It's on the sink.)"

Preview

1. Tell students that they will be asking questions to find a lost watch.
2. Direct students to look at page 102. Review the prepositions by asking students to point to the cats you describe: "Point to the cat that's next to the TV."
3. Tell students that you have a special cat in the room and that they have to find out which one it is. Write the following yes/no question pattern on the board: "Is it . . . ?" and elicit questions from students until you are sure they know the pattern.

Presentation

4. Have students look at dictionary page 28. Pick up the first 8-1/2" x 11" cue slip and do not show it to anyone. Tell students that you have hidden a watch in the living room and that they must ask you questions in order to find it. The questions must be yes/no questions that use prepositions of description and the appropriate target vocabulary. Allow students to question you

until the watch is "found." Show the cue slip.
5. Invite a volunteer to pick up one of the remaining 8-1/2" x 11" cue slips. Remind the student not to show the slip to anyone, but to tell the class which room the watch is in (The Bedroom, p. 32, or The Bathroom, p. 34). Have the class ask the volunteer yes/no questions until the watch is found.

Practice

6. Divide the class into groups of three and identify one student in each group to be the watch's "owner." Distribute the Don't Look Masks. Give each group a set of cue slips to place face-down among the group members. Explain that the watch owner will read one cue slip silently, and tell the group in which room the watch has been lost. The other two students will mask the vocabulary on the appropriate dictionary page and take turns asking yes/no questions until the watch is found. Once the watch is found, a new student becomes the owner and picks a different cue slip.
7. Direct the groups to begin, and circulate among them, monitoring the practice. Continue until all students have been owner at least once.

Follow-up

8. Ask three volunteers to step out of the room while the class hides an object (an eraser). When the students return, have them question classmates at random to locate the hidden object.

Variations

To make the activity easier, have the whole class do it together.

To make the activity more challenging, have each student owner choose any dictionary page from 27 to 35, think of a location for a watch, and write it down on a slip of scratch paper. Have the owner refer the group to the appropriate dictionary page, answer yes/no questions, and finally reveal the answer when the watch is found.

Garage Sale

Focus: Buying, selling, and negotiating at a garage sale.

Materials: Activity sheet, p. 67; Picture Cards #41–#50, p. 182; paper clips; **The Living Room, Dictionary, p. 28**

Before class, duplicate a quarter of a class set of the activity sheet. Cut apart the buyer and seller sections and keep them separate. Duplicate enough copies of the picture cards for each pair of sellers to have six items. Clip together random sets of cards. (Optional: Set up tables or desks around the room so that pairs of sellers may present their wares.)

Preview

1. Tell students that they are going to be buying or selling items at a garage sale.
2. Direct students to open their dictionaries to page 28. Ask students which items would be good for a garage sale. Write the names of the items on the board, as well as additional vocabulary from the picture cards. Mark the picture card items with an asterisk, and ask students to suggest fair prices for those in excellent, good, and poor condition.
3. Have the class practice asking for, giving, and negotiating prices: "How much is the. . . ?"; "It's. . . ."; "That's too high. How about. . . ?"

Presentation

4. Divide the class in half and assign one half the role of "buyers" and the other half the role of "sellers." Have the sellers and the buyers separately form pairs so that students can set prices or go bargain hunting as a "family."
5. Distribute a set of six picture cards and the sellers half of the activity sheet to each pair of sellers. Have partners price each item and write the price on the picture card.

6. Distribute the buyers' half of the activity sheet to the buyers and give partners a budget of $200. Using the board list, have the buyers decide what they would like to buy and how much they can spend on each item.
7. Set up a table in front of the room and write the following steps on the board:
   a. display items to sell
   b. ask for the price of an item
   c. give the price
   d. negotiate the price
   e. make the sale
   f. go to another garage sale
8. When students are ready with their prices and budget lists, invite a pair of buyers and a pair of sellers to the front of the room to negotiate a sale using whatever language resources they have.
9. Review any special language problems from the demonstration (step 8) before proceeding with the role play.

Practice

10. Have the sellers display the cards depicting the items for sale. Direct the buyers to visit as many sellers as possible in order to make the best purchases. Encourage negotiating. Begin the role play.
11. Have both buyers and sellers fill in their activity sheet under the "sold for" and "spent" columns indicating the amounts of each purchase. At the end of the activity, have students tally the amounts in the "sold for" and "spent" columns and tell the class what they bought or sold and how much money they made or spent.

Follow-up

12. Use the experiences from the role play to generate a class discussion of which sellers offered the best prices and which buyers got the best deals.

Design a Room

Focus: Designing and labeling rooms in a house.

Materials: Large sheets of butcher paper; three 8-1/2" × 11" blank sheets of paper; scissors (one pair per group); tape; colored markers; blank paper or magazines; Don't Look Mask, p. 179; **The Living Room, The Dining Room, The Kitchen, The Bedroom, The Baby's Room, The Bathroom,** and **The Utility Room, Dictionary, pp. 28–30 and 32–35.**

Before class, estimate the number of groups of four you will have for this activity and set aside that number of sheets of butcher paper. Draw the outline of three walls and a floor on each sheet. Collect the scissors, the drawing materials or magazines, and tape dispensers in equal numbers for each group. Draw the following pictures on the three 8-1/2" × 11" sheets of paper (one picture per sheet): a bed, a lamp, and a night table.

Preview

1. Tell students that they will be working in groups to design and label a room in a house, and writing a description of the "home" they have created.
2. Direct students to open their dictionaries to page 32. Distribute the Don't Look Masks and have students cover the vocabulary at the bottom of the page. Have students tell you the items they see on the page. List these items on one side of the board.

Presentation

3. Draw the outline of three walls on the board and tell students that your drawing represents a bedroom. Show students the pictures of the bed, lamp, and night table, and have students tell you where to place these items in the room: "Put the bed on the back wall." Tape these items on the board according to students' directions. Model clarification strategies, such as "On the floor or on the night table?" or "On what?"
4. Ask students to pick an item from the list on the board and to decide where it belongs. Draw the item in the bedroom. (The less perfect your drawing is, the better.) Have volunteers draw and label other items according to their classmates' directions.

Practice

5. Divide students into groups of four and have them number off 1–4. Give groups 10 minutes to decide which room they want to design, and what furnishings each student will draw or look for in the magazines.
6. After 10 minutes, have all student 1s pick up the materials their group will use. Circulate and talk to students while they are working on their designs.
7. After 20–30 minutes, have all student 2s pick up their dictionaries to check the spelling of various items in their room or to add items. (Refer students to Dictionary pages 28–30 and 32–35.)
8. After 10 more minutes, have all student 3s post the completed rooms, while student 4s collect the materials.

Follow-up

9. Tell students that their drawings represent rooms in one house. Elicit a description of this house from the class by asking questions, such as "What kind of home is this?" and "How many bedrooms docs it have?" Write the description on the board exactly as the students tell it to you. Have students read the description aloud and copy it.

    The following is a typical level-one story: This is our beautiful home. It have 4 bedrooms, 1 bathroom, a living room. It have a big yard also. There's TV and stereo in living room. There's two cockroach in the kitchen.

Your Notes

Is There Cable TV? (See Teacher's Notes, page 60.)

■ Listen to Mrs. Diego talk about different homes.
■ Make a check (√) next to the features of each home.

	Home #1	Home #2	Home #3	Home #4	Home #5
fireplace	✓				
dining room					
kitchen					
baby's room					
cable TV					
air conditioner					
dishwasher					

Garage Sale (See Teacher's Notes, page 64.)

Sellers
■ Choose six items you want to sell.
■ Price each item.

Buyers
■ List six items you want to buy.
■ Write your budget for each item.

ITEM	PRICE	SOLD FOR

ITEM	BUDGET	SPENT

Where's the Teakettle? (See Teacher's Notes, page 61.)

- Look at the kitchen picture below.
  Ask about the *blender* (1), *cutting board* (3), *colander* (5), *pot* (7), *toaster* (9), and *coffeemaker* (11).
- Write in the numbers of the missing items.
- Use this conversation as a model:
  Where's the blender?
    The what?
  The blender.
    Let's see . . . it's on the counter, next to the refrigerator.

A

- Look at the kitchen picture below.
- Ask about the *teakettle* (2), *dish towel* (4), *frying pan* (6), *dish drainer* (8), *pot holder* (10), and *canister* (12).
- Write in the numbers of the missing items.
- Use this conversation as a model:
  Where's the blender?
    The what?
  The blender.
    Let's see . . . it's on the counter, next to the refrigerator.

B

Where Does the Sofa Go? (See Teacher's Notes, page 62.)

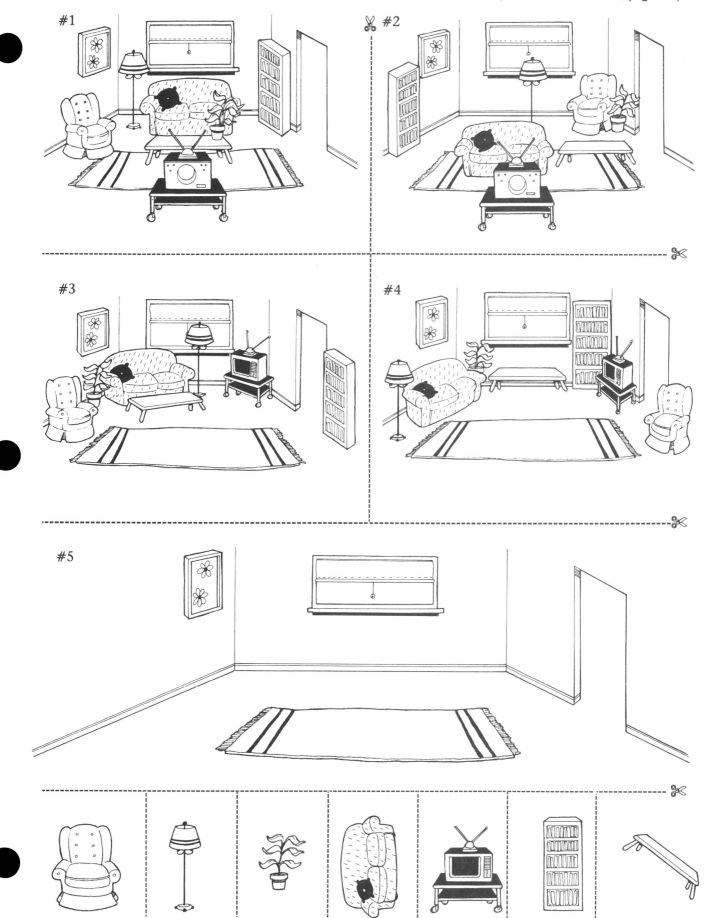

Lost and Found (See Teacher's Notes, page 63.)

READ: I lost my watch in the living room.
(It's behind the recliner.)

READ: I lost my watch in the living room.
(It's in the bookcase.)

READ: I lost my watch in the living room.
(It's on the end table.)

READ: I lost my watch in the living room.
(It's next to the fireplace.)

READ: I lost my watch in the living room.
(It's between the cushions on the sofa.)

READ: I lost my watch in the bedroom.
(It's on the floor in the closet.)

READ: I lost my watch in the bedroom.
(It's under the night table.)

READ: I lost my watch in the bedroom.
(It's on the air conditioner.)

READ: I lost my watch in the bedroom.
(It's in the jewelry box.)

READ: I lost my watch in the bedroom.
(It's next to the telephone.)

READ: I lost my watch in the bathroom.
(It's on the floor between the toilet and the scale.)

READ: I lost my watch in the bathroom.
(It's in the medicine cabinet.)

READ: I lost my watch in the bathroom.
(It's under the bath mat.)

READ: I lost my watch in the bathroom.
(It's behind the hamper.)

Working Around the Home
Teacher's Notes and Activity Sheets

A Nice Place to Live

Focus: Identifying items outside the home.

Materials: Answer Cards and Don't Look Mask, p. 179; **Houses, Dictionary, p. 27.**

Before class, duplicate and cut apart a class set of the Answer Cards and Don't Look Mask. Look over the silent drill questions and target vocabulary (step 4 below).

Preview

1. Hold up a set of answer cards and tell students that they will be listening to and answering a series of questions by raising the correct answer card.

2. Direct students to open their dictionaries to page 27. Ask students to identify the items on the page, such as lawn mower, TV antenna, rake, or garden hose. Talk about how the tools are used.

Presentation

3. Distribute the answer cards and masks. Have students cover the vocabulary at the bottom of the page and listen to your questions about pictures A, B, and C. Ask the first question: "Is the man cooking on the *grill*?" Tell students to raise the Yes card if the answer is yes, the No card if it is no, and the Not Sure card when there's not enough information to answer yes or no. Get class consensus on the first answer before continuing.

Practice

4. Ask the following questions:
   Is the man cooking on the *grill?* (Yes)
   Is the woman lying on the *lounge chair?* (No)
   Is the *wheelbarrow* filled with sand? (No)
   Is the *rake* next to the *shovel?* (Yes)
   Does the *ranch house* have a red *door?* (Yes)
   Does the *ranch house* have *shutters?* (No)
   Is there a chair on the *porch* of the *colonial-style house?* (Yes)
   Is the woman in the *hammock* happy? (Not sure)
   Is the *sprinkler* turned off? (No)
   Is the *lawn mower* next to the *watering can?* (No)

Follow-up

5. Have students talk about the differences between the ranch house and the colonial-style house. Have them draw a picture of the house or apartment they lived in as a child and describe it to the class.

A Change of Seasons

Focus: Identifying seasonal activities.

Materials: Don't Look Mask, p. 179; listening cassette; **Seasonal Verbs, Dictionary, p. 26.**

Before class, duplicate a set of the Don't Look Mask. Look over the target vocabulary in the tapescript below.

Preview

1. Tell students that they will be listening to a woman talk about seasonal chores outside her home.
2. Direct students to open their dictionaries to page 26. Mime two or three of the actions depicted on the page and have students guess what you're doing. Then invite three volunteers to come to the front of the room and have each mime a different action (planting flowers, shoveling snow, watering). Tell the class to point to the pictures in the dictionary that show a person planting flowers, shoveling snow, and so on.

Presentation

3. Distribute the masks and have students cover the vocabulary at the bottom of the page. Tell students to listen to the tape and to point to the correct pictures in their dictionaries. Assure students that they will have several opportunities to hear the listening passage.
4. Play the tape through "Yes, I know I get a backache every time I *dig*!" Stop the tape and check to be sure that students are pointing to picture #3. Replay this section of the tape until all students are pointing to picture #3.

Practice

5. Play the tape, stopping when necessary. Replay the tape two to five times.

Follow-up

6. Check for comprehension of the target vocabulary by asking questions, such as "Where is the man who's watering the flowers?" Students can respond by saying "#5" or by pointing to the correct picture.

Variation

To make the activity more challenging, have student groups write a story based on the dictionary page. Replay the tape whenever students want to clarify something they've heard.

Tapescript (with Answers)

Listen to Debbie talk about seasonal chores outside her home. Point to the items or people you hear Debbie talking about.

Oh, Mark, look! Here are some pictures that your cousin Henry took after we bought the house. Remember this one from last spring? There I am, next to our oak tree, *digging (3)* soil for my prize flowers. [pause] Yes, I know I get a backache every time I *dig (3)!* * Ian was really a big help *planting (4)* that day. See him helping me *plant (4)* the seeds?*

And there you are on the ladder *painting (1)* the house. You almost fell off, remember? You didn't *paint (1)* that garage too well, did you?* Oh, look! The grass was so green last summer! There's Ian *mowing (6)* the lawn. He needed to *mow (6)* around my flowers.* And will you take a look at those beautiful yellow flowers! Sandra wanted to *pick (7)* some for Henry's birthday, but she forgot about his allergies!* And there you are, Mark, *watering (5)* the flowers. Looks like you're about to *water (5)* Sandra. And do you see me *trimming (8)* the bushes under the window? That's when I cut my finger. What a day! [pause] Yes, Mark, I know I should wear gloves when I *trim (8)* the bushes.* Just look at all the leaves all over the ground in this picture! I got so tired *filling (9)* all those trash bags. I remember I had to *fill (9)* at least ten that day. Do you see Sandra *raking (10)* the leaves? Well, it just seemed that the more she tried to *rake (10)*, the more leaves fell!* And you, Mark, always wearing that silly red baseball cap. There you are *chopping (11)* wood. You sure can chop.* Oh, look at this one from last winter. It was so cold—snow everywhere! There's Ian *shoveling (13)* the driveway—and you know how he hates to *shovel (13)* snow.* You forgot to put the station wagon in the garage and there was ice on all the windows. There's Sandra *scraping (15)* the ice off the back window. Why didn't you *scrape (15)* the ice?* Oh you were *carrying (16)* that heavy bag. What was in there anyway? Looks like it was hard to *carry (16)*.* [pause] What do you mean we should sell the house? Too much work? Why, Mark Field, you lazy man!

Sugar on the Carpet!

> **Focus:** Identifying cleaning items.
>
> **Materials:** Activity sheet p. 81; listening cassette; **The Utility Room, Dictionary, p. 35.**
>
> *Before class, duplicate a class set of the activity sheet. Look over the target vocabulary in the tapescript below.*

Preview

1. Tell students that they will be listening to people talking about household chores.
2. Direct students to open their dictionaries to page 35. Ask the class about items used for various cleaning tasks, such as "What do you use to sweep the floor?" or "What do you use to wash clothes?"
3. Make open-ended statements, such as "My carpet is dirty. I need to use the...." "I'm going to wash my floor. I'll use a...." Elicit answers from the class.

Presentation

4. Copy number 1 (the example) from the activity sheet onto the board. Explain the task to students and assure them that they will have several opportunities to hear the listening passage.
5. Play the tape through number 1, "I spilled sugar on the carpet! Get me the...." Stop the tape and review the example on the board.
6. Distribute the activity sheets and review the directions.

Practice

7. Play the tape, stopping after each item. When necessary, replay each item two to five times.
8. Elicit students' responses for each item and get class consensus on the accuracy of the answers. Replay the tape to clarify any problems.

Follow-up

9. Have students work in pairs. Ask them to try to remember the problem each person was having by looking at their answer sheets. Get a class consensus on each item.

Tapescript (with Answers)

Listen to the people talking about household chores. Circle the item that best completes each sentence.

1. Oh, no, Jimmy. I spilled sugar on the carpet! Get me the.... *(vacuum cleaner)*
2. It's such a nice day today. I'm going to clean the windows, Marty. Please bring me the.... *(window cleaner)*
3. George, George. The power is out. I can't see a thing! Get me a.... *(flashlight)*
4. Will you look where Mommy put the cookies? I know I can reach them if you just get me the.... *(stepladder)*
5. Helen, I need to wash my shirts for my trip tomorrow. Please give me the.... *(detergent)*
6. Oh, I'm going to get in trouble now. Tommy, don't just stand there, find the.... *(broom)*
7. Did you see all the spots on Timmy's clothes? It's a good thing these pants are white. Honey, hand me the.... *(bleach)*
8. Nancy, Nancy! These clothes are blowing all over the yard. Get me some extra.... *(clothespins)*
9. You know, Dennis, I want my dress to look absolutely perfect. I already have the ironing board out. Look in the closet for the.... *(iron)*
10. Puppies are not easy. Annie, look at this mess. Quick! Get me the.... *(paper towels)*

Housework Blues

Focus: Identifying cleaning tasks.

Materials: Activity sheet, p. 81; listening cassette; **Housework and Repair Verbs, Dictionary, p. 38.**

Before class, duplicate a class set of the activity sheet and look over the target vocabulary in the tapescript below.

Preview

1. Tell students that they will be listening to people talk about cleaning their homes and will number the tasks in the order they hear them described.
2. Have students open their dictionaries to page 38 and look over the housework and repair verbs. Elicit the names of cleaning tasks that students might do on a typical cleaning day, such as wash the dishes or vacuum the carpet. Write students' responses on the board.
3. Ask different students to number the tasks in the order in which they would do them. Write the numbers next to the verbs.

Presentation

4. Copy letter A (the example) from the activity sheet onto the board. Explain the task to students, and assure them that they will have several opportunities to hear the listening passage.
5. Play the tape through the first household task ". . . and I *change all the sheets,*" and review the example on the board.
6. Distribute the activity sheets and review the directions.

Practice

7. Play the tape, stopping after each item. Replay an item two to five times, pausing between the household tasks when necessary.
8. Elicit students' responses for each order and get consensus on the accuracy of the

answers. Replay the tape to clarify any problems.

Follow-up

9. Teach student clarification questions for this situation, such as "And then what do you do?" or "What do you do next?"
10. Have students write down the tasks they do on a typical cleaning day and the order in which they do them. Pair students and have them share their lists with their partner.

Tapescript (with Answers)

Listen to people talk about cleaning their homes. Number the tasks as you hear them described. Some tasks may not be mentioned.

A. How do I clean my apartment? Well, I do it on Saturdays. I start in the bedroom and I *change all the sheets (1)*. Then, of course, while I'm there, I *make the beds (2)*. I must *vacuum the carpets (3)* because I have two dogs. When I'm done with that, I have something to eat. After I eat, I *wash the dishes (4)* and *dry (5)* them. That pretty much does it.

B. I get my family to help—that's how I clean. First, my youngest son and daughter *make the beds (1)*. Then we all have a nice breakfast and my husband *washes (2)* and *dries (3)* the dishes. The little ones go out to play while the oldest son *vacuums the carpet (4)*. After lunch my oldest daughter *scrubs the kitchen floor (5)* and then she helps me *do the laundry (6)*.

C. My wife and I clean the house together—takes half the time that way. First we *change the sheets (1)* and *make the bed (2)*. Then I *vacuum the carpet (3)* in the living room. She doesn't like the noise so she goes out back and *does the laundry (4)*. When the laundry is done, we go into the kitchen. I *wash the dishes (5)* and she *dries (6)* them. This week no one scrubbed the floors! Maybe next time!

D. Clean, huh? Well, I don't do much. I *wash the dishes (1)*, but I don't dry them. Then I *change the sheets (2)* on the bed, but I don't make it. I never vacuum and I never scrub the floors. I guess that's it.

E. I think there is really only one way to clean. Do what you don't like first. I *do all the laundry (1)* in the laundry basket. After that, I *wash the dishes (2)*. When the dishes are done, I *scrub the floors (3)*—get right down on my knees, too. Next, I *vacuum the carpet (4)*. I actually like to vacuum. Then I *change the bed sheets (5)*. I don't make the bed, because by that time I'm ready to get into it!

Tools Plus

> **Focus:** Asking for and giving the location of items in a hardware store.
>
> **Materials:** Activity sheet, p. 82; manila folders (one per pair); **The Utility Room,** and **A Workshop, Dictionary, pp. 35–37.**
>
> ---
>
> *Before class, duplicate half a class set of the activity sheet. Cut apart the A and B sections of the sheets and keep them separate. Copy the conversation and store department headings from the activity sheet onto the board.*

Preview

1. Tell students that they will be working in pairs to find out the location of items on a store directory.
2. Direct students to open their dictionaries to pages 35, 36, and 37 and to look at the pictures. Ask students which of the depicted items they have in their homes and in which store departments they could find them. Write this information on the board under the appropriate headings (appliances, tools, housewares). Add random aisle numbers next to several items.

Presentation

3. Use the conversation on the board to model the language and clarification strategy you want students to use in the activity. Have the class practice the conversation, substituting different hardware store items.
4. Pair students and assign each one an A or a B role. Explain to students that they will each have a store directory with some aisle numbers missing. Point out that the missing information is on their partner's directory. Tell students that they will take turns asking for and giving this missing information in order to complete their directories.
5. Distribute a manila folder to each pair, to be propped up between the students as a screen. Distribute the A and B activity sheets

to the appropriate partners. Instruct students to look only at their own papers and not at their partner's.
6. Tell students to look at the example on their directories and to tell you the location of the hammer. Check comprehension by asking A students, "Where can I find a laundry basket?" Ask B students, "Where can I find an iron?"
7. Have one pair demonstrate the activity by asking for and giving one additional piece of missing information. Remind students to look only at their own papers.

Practice

8. Have students, in pairs, ask and answer questions about the missing information on their activity sheets. Once they complete the task, partners can compare directories to be sure they are the same.

Follow-up

9. Have pairs form groups of four to add five other items, one from each department, to their directories. Tell students to use pages 35–37 in their dictionaries and their completed directories as reference.

We Can Fix It

Focus: Solving repair problems.

Materials: Activity sheet, p. 83; 8-1/2" x 11" blank sheets of paper; **A Workshop, Dictionary, pp. 36–37.**

Before class, duplicate three copies of the activity sheet. (If you have more than 30 students, duplicate additional copies.) Each student will receive one cue slip. Copy the following sentences onto four 8-1/2" x 11" sheets of paper (one on each page): "I can paint a peeling wall." (two copies); "I can hang a light fixture."; and "I can replace a door."

Preview

1. Tell students that they will be working as a group to decide what tools they need to make repairs in the house.
2. Ask students for examples of household repairs and list their suggestions on the board. Be sure to include one or two examples from the activity sheet.
3. Direct students to open their dictionaries to pages 36 and 37. Have students tell you which tools are needed for the repair jobs listed on the board.

Presentation

4. Copy the following conversation onto the board: Student 1: "Can you paint a peeling wall?" Student 2: "Yes I can." (or) "No, I can't. I can replace a door." Model this conversation with the class and substitute other repair jobs listed on the board.
5. Invite four volunteers to the front of the room and give each one an 8-1/2" x 11" cue slip. Have the volunteers show the class their cue slips and ask one another questions based on what their cue slips say. When the two volunteers with the "peeling wall" cue slips find each other, have them brainstorm the names of the tools they need to do the repair job. Write the names of the tools on the board, adding, if necessary, suggestions from the class.

Practice

6. Distribute the cue slips and explain that students will need to circulate to find other classmates with the same cue-slip information. Once students have found one another, they become a group. Give each group a blank sheet of paper on which students can list the tools they need to complete the group's particular job. Students may consult their dictionaries while making the lists.
7. As the groups finish, distribute more blank paper and have the groups exchange repair problems so that each group has a new repair job. Continue until time runs out.

Follow-up

8. At the end of the activity, discuss each household repair job, the tools, and hardware items chosen.

Variations

To make this activity easier, discuss each household repair problem with the class and have the class brainstorm a list of tools needed to complete the repair job.

To make this activity more challenging, have students, in groups, list the tools and then list the steps they would follow to complete the repair job.

Housework Survey

> **Focus:** Discussing housework responsibilities.
>
> **Materials:** Activity sheet, p. 83; **Seasonal Verbs,** and **Housework and Repair Verbs, Dictionary, pp. 26 and 38.**
>
> ─────────────────────
>
> *Before class, duplicate a class set of the activity sheet.*

Preview

1. Tell students that they will be interviewing their classmates and talking about housework responsibilities.
2. Direct students to open their dictionaries to pages 26 and 38. Ask students to name the household chores that are done every day, once a week, once a month, and so on. Ask students which family member in their household does those chores. Write students' answers on the board. (Review the names of family relationships if necessary.)

Presentation

3. Copy the grid from the activity sheet onto the board. Model "who" questions for each space on the grid: "Who washes the dishes?"; "Who works in the yard?"; and so on. Using the grid on the board, write your name in the first column and have the class ask you the first question. Answer the question about your family and write your answer in the grid box. Explain that only short answers are written in the boxes below the questions.
4. Ask a volunteer to come to the board. Write the student's name under your name on the grid. Have different students ask the volunteer one question each from the grid. Write the answers on the grid.

Practice

5. Divide the class into groups of five and distribute an activity sheet to each student.
6. Have students take turns asking the questions of the person on their left, while the other group members listen and write the answers on their grids. When students have completed their grids, they can use the information to discuss the questions at the bottom of the activity sheet.
7. Set a 20-minute time limit for students to complete the task. Circulate and monitor student practice.

Follow-up

8. Use the grid on the board to elicit responses from each group. Number the groups and write the group numbers in the first column. Ask the survey questions and write the groups' responses on the board. Continue asking the groups all the questions, writing the single majority response wherever possible. If each group member has a different answer, write "varies."
9. When you've finished interviewing all the groups, have students use your completed survey to comment on patterns in the class.

Variations

To make the activity easier, conduct a teacher-directed survey with the whole class.

To make the activity more challenging, have groups generate three additional items to include in their surveys.

May I Borrow a Hammer?

Focus: Matching tools and household items with their functions.

Materials: Activity sheet, p. 84; four 8-1/2" x 11" blank sheets of paper; paper clips; **The Utility Room,** and **A Workshop, Dictionary, pp. 35–37.**

Before class, duplicate one copy of the activity sheet. You will need a matching set of cue slips for every two students in your class. (If you have more than 28 students, duplicate two copies of the activity sheet.) Cut apart the cue slips, keeping the borrower and lender slips separate with paper clips. Copy the following words and phrases onto the four 8-1/2" x 11" sheets of paper (one word or phrase per sheet): "The floor is dirty. (bucket and mop)," "A bucket and a mop," "The sinks are dirty. (cleanser)," and "Cleanser."

Preview

1. Tell students that they are going to borrow from or lend items to people in "their neighborhood."
2. Direct students to open their dictionaries to pages 35, 36, and 37. Ask students for examples of household items and tools, and their uses. Be sure to include all the items mentioned on the activity sheet. Ask students which items they would be willing to lend to a neighbor. Talk about borrowing and returning items and tools.

Presentation

3. Copy the following conversation onto the board: Student 1: "I have a problem. The floor is dirty. May I borrow a bucket and a mop?" Student 2: "Yes, of course." (or) "No, I'm sorry. Do you need cleanser?" (from the cue slip). Model the conversation for the class. Then have the class practice it, substituting other problems and responses.

4. Invite four volunteers to the front of the room and give each an 8-1/2" x 11" cue slip. Have the volunteers show the class their cue slips.
5. Have the volunteers practice the conversation. When the borrower finds the right tool or household item for the task, he asks to borrow it. The lenders give their cue slips to the borrowers, who return to their seats.

Practice

6. Randomly distribute the cue slips and have students circulate to find their match. When a borrower finds the right tools or household items, he takes the cue slip from the lender and sits down.

Follow-up

7. After the mixer is completed, discuss with students borrowing practices in their native countries. Talk about what items are difficult to lend to others.

Variation

To make the activity more challenging, have lenders go back to the borrowers and ask them to return the various tools and items.

Your Notes

Sugar on the Carpet! (See Teacher's Notes, page 74.)

■ Listen to the people talking about household chores.
■ Circle the item that best completes each sentence.

1. iron	vacuum cleaner	flashlight
2. dustpan	mop	window cleaner
3. flashlight	bucket	feather duster
4. dryer	broom	stepladder
5. paper towels	detergent	cleanser
6. broom	washing machine	detergent
7. ironing board	bleach	mousetrap
8. paper towels	fabric softener	clothespins
9. iron	rags	garbage can
10. laundry	spray starch	paper towels

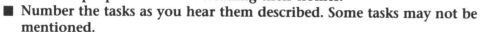

Housework Blues (See Teacher's Notes, page 75.)

■ Listen to people talk about cleaning their homes.
■ Number the tasks as you hear them described. Some tasks may not be mentioned.

Tools Plus (See Teacher's Notes, page 76.)

- Ask and answer questions about the location of these items:
  hammers, irons, washing machines, grounding plugs, lightbulbs, brooms, rollers, screwdrivers.
- Write in the missing aisle numbers.
- Use this conversation as a model:
  Where can I find a hammer?
     Tools, aisle 4.
  Aisle what?
     Aisle 4.

A

TOOLS PLUS DIRECTORY

Appliances	Electrical	Housewares	Paint	Tools
Irons Aisle ____	Extension Cords Aisle 2	Brooms Aisle ____	Paintbrushes Aisle 5	Hammers Aisle 4
Vacuum Cleaners Aisle 8	Grounding Plugs Aisle ____	Ironing Boards Aisle 10	Pans Aisle 6	Pliers Aisle 5
Washing Machines Aisle ____	Lightbulbs Aisle ____	Laundry Baskets Aisle 9	Rollers Aisle ____	Screwdrivers Aisle ____

- Look at the directory below.
- Ask and answer questions about the locations of these items:
  hammers, vacuum cleaners, extension cords, ironing boards, laundry baskets, paintbrushes, pans, pliers.
- Write in the missing aisle numbers.
- Use this conversation as a model:
  Where can I find a hammer?
     Tools, aisle 4.
  Aisle what?
     Aisle 4.

B

TOOLS PLUS DIRECTORY

Appliances	Electrical	Housewares	Paint	Tools
Irons Aisle 7	Extension Cords Aisle ____	Brooms Aisle 12	Paintbrushes Aisle ____	Hammers Aisle 4
Vacuum Cleaners Aisle ____	Grounding Plugs Aisle 2	Ironing Boards Aisle ____	Pans Aisle ____	Pliers Aisle ____
Washing Machines Aisle 11	Lightbulbs Aisle 1	Laundry Baskets Aisle ____	Rollers Aisle 6	Screwdrivers Aisle 3

We Can Fix It (See Teacher's Notes, page 77.)

I can fix a leaky pipe.	I can replace a wall switch.
I can pull out nails from a wall.	I can hang a picture.
I can refinish an old chair.	I can fix a broken window.
I can replace a plug on a lamp.	I can replace a door.
I can hang a light fixture.	I can replace curtain rods.

Housework Survey (See Teacher's Notes, page 78.)

- Work in small groups.
- Take turns asking and answering the questions on the grid below.
- Record the answers on the grid.

NAME	Who washes the dishes?	Who repairs broken things?	Who does the laundry?	Who scrubs the bathroom?	Who sweeps the floors?

- After you complete the grid, discuss these questions with your group:
  In general, is there a difference between men's and women's responsibilities?
  Is there a household chore that is never done?
  Is there a least favorite chore?
  Who in the house does the most work?

May I Borrow a Hammer? (See Teacher's Notes, page 79.)

Borrowers

✂

The carpet is dirty. (a vacuum and attachments)

✂

I can't reach the light fixtures. (a stepladder)

✂

The windows are dirty. (window cleaner and rags)

✂

The toilet is stopped up. (a plunger)

✂

The light fixtures have no lightbulbs. (lightbulbs)

✂

The kitchen floor is dusty. (a broom and dustpan)

✂

The sinks are dirty. (cleanser)

✂

I want to put on new switch plates. (a screwdriver and screws)

✂

There is old paint on the shelves. (a scraper)

✂

A mouse is running through a closet. (mousetrap)

✂

I want to measure the living room. (a tape measure)

✂

The window sill is broken. (hammer and nails)

✂

The faucet is leaking. (monkey wrench and washers)

✂

The picture-frame wire is broken. (wire and pliers)

Lenders

✂

vacuum and attachments	a stepladder	window cleaner and rags	a broom and dustpan	lightbulbs

✂

a plunger	cleanser	a scraper	a mousetrap	a tape measure

✂

screwdriver and screws	hammer and nails	monkey wrench and washers		wire and pliers

✂

Taking Care of Your Health
Teacher's Notes and Activity Sheets

Reproducible activity sheets on pages 95–98.

Ouch! That Hurts!

Focus: Identifying activities in a medical and dental office.

Materials: Answer Cards and Don't Look Mask, p. 179; **Medical and Dental Care, Dictionary, p. 39.**

Before class, duplicate and cut apart a class set of the Answer Cards and Don't Look Mask. Look over the silent drill questions and the target vocabulary (step 4 below).

Preview

1. Hold up a set of answer cards and tell students that they will be listening to and answering a series of questions by raising the correct answer card.
2. Direct students to open their dictionaries to page 39. Ask students to identify the people in the pictures (nurse, dentist, patients, attendants). Talk about what they are doing.

Presentation

3. Distribute the answer cards and masks. Have students cover the vocabulary at the bottom of the page and listen to your questions about the pictures. Ask the first question: "Is there a *patient* on the *examining table*?" Tell students to raise the Yes card if the answer is yes, the No card if it is no, and the Not Sure card when there's not enough information to answer yes or no. Get class consensus on the first answer before continuing.

Practice (with Answers)

4. Ask the following questions:
   Is there a *patient* on the *examining table?* (Yes)
   Is the *doctor* friendly? (Not Sure)
   Is there an *attendant* in the *wheelchair?* (No)
   Is the dentist holding the *needle?* (No)
   Is there a *basin* in the *dental office?* (Yes)
   Is there a *crutch* on the *stretcher?* (No)
   Is there a *cast* on the patient's arm? (No)
   Is the *oral hygienist* helping the *doctor?* (No)
   Is the *nurse* talking? (Not Sure)
   Is the *Band-Aid* on the patient's arm? (Yes)

Follow-up

5. Have students talk about the conversations that might be taking place. Ask students to identify the people and what each person is saying.

It's an Emergency!

> **Focus:** Identifying fire emergency vocabulary.
>
> **Materials:** Don't Look Mask, p. 179; listening cassette; **Firefighting and Rescue, Dictionary, p. 42.**
>
> *Before class, duplicate a class set of the Don't Look Mask. Look over the target vocabulary in the tapescript below.*

Preview

1. Tell students that they will be listening to a news reporter describe an emergency.
2. Direct students to open their dictionaries to page 42. Ask the class to identify emergency and safety equipment. Elicit several uses for each item and write students' suggestions on the board.

Presentation

3. Distribute the masks and have students cover the vocabulary at the bottom of the page. Tell students to listen to the tape and to point to the correct pictures in their dictionaries. Assure students that they will have several opportunities to hear the listening passage.
4. Play the tape through *"Fire engines are arriving and pulling up next to the building."* Stop the tape and check to be sure that students are pointing to picture #2. Replay this section of the tape until all students are pointing to picture #2.

Practice

5. Play the tape, stopping when necessary. Replay the tape two to five times.

Follow-up

6. Check for comprehension of the target vocabulary by asking questions, such as "Who is helping the man on the ground?" Students can respond by saying "#7" or by pointing to the correct picture.

Variation

To make the follow-up more challenging, have students, in pairs, brainstorm prevention and first aid strategies in one of the following situations: earthquake, auto accident, or fire.

Tapescript (with Answers)

Listen to Anna Vargas talk about a fire in an apartment building. Point to the correct items or people.

Good evening. This is Anna Vargas reporting live from downtown. We're on the scene of a terrible tragedy at the Westchester Apartments. *Fire engines (2)* are arriving and pulling up next to the building.* *Smoke (15)* is filling the street and it's really hard to breathe. [cough cough]* Emergency workers have just hooked up the *hose (8)*. They've attached it to the *fire hydrant (9)* in order to control this blaze.* One of the *fire fighters* is carrying an *ax (14)* and is going around the back of the building.* Another one is going towards the front entrance with a *fire extinguisher (11)*. He's going to try to get into the building.* He needs to get up to the second story. Maybe he can use that *ladder (1)*. It's on the *fire truck (3)* now.* You can see the *fire (5)* in the second story window. The flames are really hot.* Luckily, most residents used the *fire escape (4)* to get out of the building.* Unfortunately, one man in that second story apartment panicked and jumped out of the window. He's lying in the street. A *paramedic (7)* is working on him right now.* It's a good thing that his neighbor called 911 immediately. An *ambulance (6)* is ready to transport him to a local hospital.* At this time, we don't know the cause of this fire, but we'll keep you informed with our News at Seven. This is Anna Vargas, Action News.

Dr. Segal's Busy Day

> **Focus:** Categorizing ailments and treatments.
>
> **Materials:** Activity sheet, p. 95; listening cassette; **Medical and Dental Care, Ailments and Injuries,** and **Treatments and Remedies, Dictionary, pp. 39–41.**
>
> *Before class, duplicate a class set of the activity sheet and look over the target vocabulary in the tapescript below.*

Preview

1. Tell students that they will be listening to a nurse informing a doctor of his schedule for the day.
2. Direct students to open their dictionaries to pages 40 and 41. Review the vocabulary associated with medical ailments and injuries (p. 40). Write the following phrases on the board: "I have a. . . ." "I need. . . ." Model the first phrase as you mime one of the ailments depicted on the page, and have students guess what you're doing. Then invite three volunteers to the front of the class. Have each volunteer mime a different ailment or injury for the class. Write students' answers on the board under the first phrase.
3. Use the students' sentences from step 2 to review the vocabulary associated with treatments and remedies (p. 41). Model the second phrase as you mime one of the ailments, and have students identify appropriate treatments. Write students' responses under the second phrase.

Presentation

4. Copy the two category headings, Ailment/ Injury and Treatment/Remedy, from the activity sheet onto the board. Explain the task to the students, and assure them that they will have several opportunities to hear the listening passage.
5. Play the tape through "He has a terrible *stomachache,*" and review the example.

6. Distribute the activity sheets and review the directions.

Practice

7. Play the tape, stopping when necessary.
8. Take a survey of the number of checks made under each category. Get class consensus on the accuracy of the numbers. If class response is inaccurate, have students repeat the activity using the second set of categories (B). When necessary, replay the tape a third time using the third set of categories (C).
9. Invite a volunteer to do the activity on the board as you play the tape one last time.

Follow-up

10. Have students, in groups of three, brainstorm a list of treatments and remedies for the following conditions: headache, stomachache, sore throat, and high blood pressure. Encourage use of the dictionary vocabulary as well as vocabulary for other therapies.

Tapescript (with Answers)

Listen to the nurse talk about medical appointments. Make a check in the correct box.

Hello, Dr. Segal? This is Christina Pérez at Glenbrook Medical Center. I'm calling with your schedule. Let's see. Your first patient, Andrew Dunn, will be here at 9:15. He has a terrible *stomachache.** At 9:45, you'll see Jorge Santos. He's got *high blood pressure* and would like you to check it. He needs a refill on his *pills.** At 10:30, you have a new patient, Anna Cho. Says her doctor recommends *surgery* for her *backache.* Hmm . . . sounds like she wants a second opinion.* Your 11:30 patient just cancelled—said he had a bad *bruise* from falling off a bicycle, but he's OK now.* Looks like you're free until after lunch . . . Oh, please don't forget to call in those prescriptions for Mrs. Jordan's *eye drops* and Mr. Berger's *ointment.** You only have two appointments this afternoon. Maggie Howard is bringing her twins, Danielle and Harry. Harry's got a *sore throat, chills,* and a *high fever.* Everyone at day care has the same thing.* Danielle's got a *cut* on her thumb, but I don't think she'll need *stitches.* It's her left thumb . . . When? Oh, that's at 2:30.* Your last patient is at 3:45. Albert Cruz needs a *cast* on his arm. He fell while helping his pregnant wife move furniture. Yes, she's on *bed rest* and can't do any moving.* Mr. Klein called to ask you about his *toothache* . . . What? Yes, Dr. Segal, I told him you're not a dentist!

(**Answers:** Ailment/Injury—9 checks; Treatment/Remedy—7 checks)

Bodybuilding

> **Focus:** Identifying the parts of the human body.
>
> **Materials:** Activity sheet p. 96; listening cassette; Don't Look Mask, p. 179; **The Human Body, Dictionary, pp. 4–5.**
> ___
>
> *Before class, duplicate a class set of the activity sheet and the Don't Look Mask. Look over the target vocabulary in the tapescript below. Write the following vocabulary on the board: chin, ring finger, tongue, ankle.*

Preview

1. Tell students that they will be following directions to put letters on parts of the hand, head, foot, and other parts of the body.
2. Direct students to open their dictionaries to pages 4 and 5. Distribute the Don't Look Masks and have students cover the vocabulary and look over the pictures on the pages. Point to the word "chin" on the board and have students find it on the male figure on page 4. Ask students to tell you the corresponding number (#3), then have them brainstorm different ways to describe the location of the chin, such as "It's below the mouth." "It's above the neck." Continue this process with the remaining three words on the board.

Presentation

3. Copy the head in number 1 (the example) from the activity sheet onto the board. Explain the task to students, and assure them that they will have several opportunities to hear the listening passage.
4. Play the tape through number 1, "Put an A on the lower *lip*," and review the example. Call out the parts of the body and have students tell you the corresponding letters.
5. Distribute the activity sheets and review the directions with the class.

Practice

6. Play the tape, stopping after each item. When necessary, replay each item two to five times.
7. Have students, in pairs, compare their completed activity sheets to see if their letters match. Write the letters and vocabulary for each item on the board, as the students dictate them to you.

Follow-up

8. Have students unscramble the four letters for each item on their activity sheets and identify the vocabulary. Invite volunteers to write the words on the board.
9. Have the class construct a body on the board, part by part. Draw the outline of a head on the board. Have a volunteer take the chalk from you and draw the next part of the body according to your directions, "Draw two eyes in the center." Ask the volunteer to give the chalk to another student and tell him what to draw and where to draw it. Students continue drawing and giving directions until the body is completed.

___

Tapescript (with Answers)

Listen to the directions. Put a letter on the correct part of the body.

1. Put an R on the *forehead*. Put an H on the *ear*. Put an I above the *mouth*, on the *nose*. Put an A on the lower *lip*. (H-A-I-R)
2. Put a D between the *shoulder* and the *chin*, on the *neck*. Put an O between the *forearm* and the *upper arm*, on the *elbow*. Put a Y on the *chest*. Put a B between the *abdomen* and the *chest*, on the *waist*. (B-O-D-Y)
3. Put an A on the *wrist*. Put an N between the *wrist* and the *middle finger*, on the *palm*. Put a D on the *thumb*. Put an H next to the *ring finger*, on the *little finger*. (H-A-N-D)
4. Put an O on the *heel*. Put a T above the *heel*, on the *ankle*. Put an S on the *toenail*. Put an E on the *big toe*. (T-O-E-S)
5. Put an E under the *ear*, on the *jaw*. Put an N inside the *mouth*, on the *tongue*. Put an S between the *nose* and the *ear*, on the *cheek*. Put an O on the *beard*. (N-O-S-E)

Take Two Aspirin

Focus: Asking for and giving information on medicine labels.

Materials: Activity sheet, p. 97; manila folders (one per pair); **Treatments and Remedies,** and **Appendix, Dictionary, pp. 41 and 104.**

Before class, duplicate half a class set of the activity sheet. Cut apart the A and B sections of the sheets and keep them separate. Copy the questions from the activity sheet onto the board.

Preview

1. Tell students that they will be working in pairs to find out the missing information on medicine labels.
2. Direct students to open their dictionaries to page 41. Have students brainstorm the kinds of medicines they use and the name, purpose, and dosage of each one. Draw a sample medicine label on the board including the product's name and what it treats. Have the class tell you what other information they'd expect to see on the label. Write the information on the label. (Be sure to include dosage and expiration date.)

Presentation

3. Use the questions on the board to model the language and clarification strategy you want students to use in the activity. Have the class practice asking and answering the questions for the sample medicine label.
4. Pair students and assign each one an A or a B role. Explain to students that they will each have medicine labels with some information missing. Point out that the missing information is on their partner's medicine labels. Tell students that they will take turns asking for and giving information in order to fill in their labels.

5. Distribute a manila folder to each pair, to be propped up between the students as a screen. Distribute the A and B activity sheets to the appropriate partners. Review the directions and instruct students to look only at their own papers and not at their partner's.
6. Tell students to look at medicine label #1 and to tell you the dosage for Care Aspirin. Check comprehension by asking A students, "When do you discard Care Aspirin?" Ask B students, "Why do you take Care Aspirin?"
7. Have one pair demonstrate the activity by asking for and giving information from their medicine labels. Remind students to look only at their own labels.

Practice

8. Have students, in pairs, ask and answer questions about the missing information on their medicine labels. Once they complete the task, partners can compare labels to be sure they are the same.

Follow-up

9. Have pairs form groups of four to create a medicine. (Students can use page 41 in their dictionaries for reference.) Each group then presents its medicine in a "TV commercial" using the following conversation:
Student 1: What's the matter? Student 2: I have a _____. Student 1: Here, try some _____. It's great for _____. Student 2: (tries some) Hey! I feel much better, thanks to _____. It really works!

Accidents Happen

Focus: Describing the sequence of events in an accident.

Materials: Activity sheet, p. 95; Picture Cards #63, #131, #138, and #140, p. 183 and p. 186; four 8-1/2" x 11" blank sheets of paper; paper clips; **Medical and Dental Care, Ailments and Injuries, Treatments and Remedies,** and **Firefighting and Rescue, Dictionary, pp. 39–42.**

Before class, duplicate one-sixth of a class set of the activity sheet. Cut apart the pictures, scramble each set, and clip the sets together. Copy the four Picture Cards—#63 (backache), #131 (lie down), #138 (lift), and #140 (take medicine)—onto the four 8-1/2" x 11" sheets of paper (one picture per sheet). Draw a heating pad (a rectangle with a wiggly line coming out of it) under the man in picture #131. Write the numbers 1–4 across the board.

Preview

1. Tell students that they will be working in groups to sequence six pictures that tell the story of an accident in the home.
2. Direct students to open their dictionaries to page 40. Have students locate the woman with a cold (#11). Using *Wh-* questions, such as "Why does she have a cold?"; "What will she do?"; and "What is she doing?", ask students to describe what happened before, during, and after the ailment. Write students' responses on the board. Have the class reach consensus on the sequencing of the different activities.

Presentation

3. Invite four volunteers to the front of the room. Give each student one of the 8-1/2" x 11" pictures. Tell the volunteers not to show their pictures to the class. Have the volunteers describe what's happening in their pictures. Using the numbers 1–4 on the

board, have the class tell you the order in which each of the students should stand: first, second, third, or fourth, based on the action in their pictures. Ask the volunteers to stand in that order and to reveal their pictures. Have the class decide if the sequence is correct.

Practice

4. Divide the class into groups of six and tell students that they will each be getting one picture from a set of six. Point out that they must conceal their pictures from their fellow group members. Explain that students will take turns describing their pictures. Then each student will repeat her description, and the group will decide where that particular picture fits into the sequence 1–6.
5. Distribute the picture sets to each group, one picture per student.
6. Set a 15-minute time limit for students, but increase the time if necessary.
7. Once the time is up, describe one picture at a time in order. See if students challenge or agree with your sequence. Ask for volunteers to describe any other possible sequences.

Follow-up

8. Have the class dictate the accident story to you as you write it on the board. Give students time to copy it.

Variations

To make this activity easier, use the activity sheet with the picture cards in sequence to guide students in telling the story.

To make this activity more challenging, have students add to the original picture story or create a different ending.

Is the Doctor In?

Focus: Matching ailments and injuries with their remedies

Materials: Activity sheet, p. 96; Picture Cards #61–70, p. 183; four 8-1/2″ x 11″ blank sheets of paper; paper clips; **Ailments and Injuries,** and **Treatments and Remedies, Dictionary, pp. 40–41.**

Before class, duplicate two copies of the activity sheet, cut apart the cue slips, and mix them up. Duplicate two copies of the Picture Cards, cut them apart, mix them up, and set them aside. You will need a matching set of one cue slip and one picture card for every two students. (If you have more than 40 students, duplicate extra copies of the activity sheet and picture cards.) Copy the following instruction onto two of the 8-1/2″ x 11″ sheets of paper: "Drink hot tea with lemon and don't talk so much," "Use a heating pad, get bed rest, and don't lift heavy things." Draw the following pictures on the remaining two 8-1/2″ x 11″ sheets: a backache and a sore throat. (Use Picture Cards #63 and #65 for reference.)

Preview

1. Tell students that they will be asking for and giving medical advice.
2. Direct students to open their dictionaries to page 40. Point out the illustration of a sore throat (#12), and ask students what remedies they would suggest for this ailment. List the remedies on the board. Follow the same procedure using other ailments, being sure to cover all the ailments and remedies used in the mixer.

Presentation

3. Copy the following conversation onto the board:
   Student 1: "I have a sore throat. What I can do for it?"

   Student 2: "Drink hot tea with lemon and don't talk so much!"
   Have the class practice the conversation, substituting different ailments and remedies. Be sure to model, "Sorry, I don't know," as an alternative response.
4. Put four chairs in the front of the room, invite four volunteers to the front, and give each an 8-1/2″ x 11″ picture or an 8-1/2″ x 11″ cue slip. Don't have the volunteers sit down. Ask them to show their pictures or cue slips to the class. Have the volunteers practice the conversation (as in step 3). When the volunteers are matched up, have them sit down together. Tell students that when they sit down with their match, they will list all the remedies they can think of for their ailment.

Practice

5. Divide the class in half. Randomly distribute the cue slips to one half and the picture cards to the other. Have the students with the ailment picture cards use the model conversation (step 3) to look for students holding cue slips with a matching remedy. When students find their match, have them sit down in pairs and together list the other remedies for the same problem. Circulate and monitor student practice.

Follow-up

6. After the mixer is completed, have the class brainstorm cultural remedies for each of the ailments from the mixer. Encourage students to share the most interesting or strangest remedies they've heard of.

Variations

To make the practice easier, identify the matching ailments and remedies before students look for their partners.

To make the follow-up more challenging, have students visit a pharmacy and get advice for any of the ailments on the picture cards: "I have a headache. What I can do for it?"

Health Fair

Focus: Asking for and giving personal health statistics.

Materials: Activity sheet, p. 98; seven sheets of construction paper; seven markers; a yard stick; a bathroom scale; an eye chart or an 8-1/2″ × 14″ sheet of blank paper; a watch with a second hand; **The Human Body,** and **Ailments and Injuries, Dictionary, pp. 4–5 and 40.**

Before class, duplicate a class set of the activity sheet. Copy the headings from the activity sheet onto the board (Registration, Height, Weight, and so on). Include the registration and interview information under the appropriate headings. Next to the Height heading, draw a chart marking 4 feet through 6-1/2 feet, inch by inch. Use a real eye chart (or one drawn on the 8-1/2″ × 14″ sheet of paper) and post it under the Vision heading.

Preview

1. Tell students that they will be doctors and patients at a health fair.
2. Direct students to open their dictionaries to page 40 and to look at #10. Ask students how often they get their blood pressure checked. Talk about what happens during a check-up.

Presentation

3. Assume the role of doctor and have volunteers role play your patients. Demonstrate the language and equipment students will use at each health fair station: Registration (health fair form)—"Mr. Julio Sanchez? Go to station 1."; Weight (scale)—"Stand on the scale."; Height (height chart)—"Stand up straight."; Vision (eye chart)—"Cover your right eye and read line four."; Pulse (watch)—"Run in place for one minute."; Reflexes (table)—"Sit here."
4. Model the questions under the Interview

heading on the board. Ask the class to suggest possible responses for each question. Erase the board.
5. Divide the class into doctors (15 students), receptionists (3 students), and patients (remaining students). Explain that the patients will register with the receptionists and then go to the different doctors' stations.
6. Group doctors in threes and assign each group one of the six stations. Distribute the materials (see step 3) and markers and construction paper for making signs. Distribute the activity sheets to the patients and have them fill out the upper portion using page 40 as reference. Have the receptionists fill out an activity sheet as well, and explain that when they have finished registering students, they will join the role play as patients.
7. Collect the activity sheets and put the following steps on the board:
   a. greet patient
   b. state problem
   c. collect forms
   d. follow doctor's directions
   e. examine patient
   f. record information
   g. go to next station
   Have the students look at these steps to see what they will be doing during the role play. Point out that the activity sheet will also guide them in the role play.
8. Create six stations in your classroom and direct all doctors to their stations. Circulate as a patient and have the doctors at each station practice on you. Review any special language problems from the demonstration (step 7) before proceeding with the role play.

Practice

9. Direct the receptionists and patients to the Registration area. Give the receptionists the activity sheets and have them call out patients' names, six at a time, until all patients are at a station.
10. Circulate and monitor practice. When a patient completes her form, she may switch roles with one of the doctors. End the role play when all forms are completed.

Your Notes

Dr. Segal's Busy Day (See Teacher's Notes, page 88.)

- Listen to the nurse talk about medical appointments.
- Make a check (√) in the correct box.

A.	B.	C.
✔		
Ailment/Injury	Ailment/Injury	Ailment/Injury
Treatment/Remedy	Treatment/Remedy	Treatment/Remedy

--- ✂

Accidents Happen (See Teacher's Notes, page 91.)

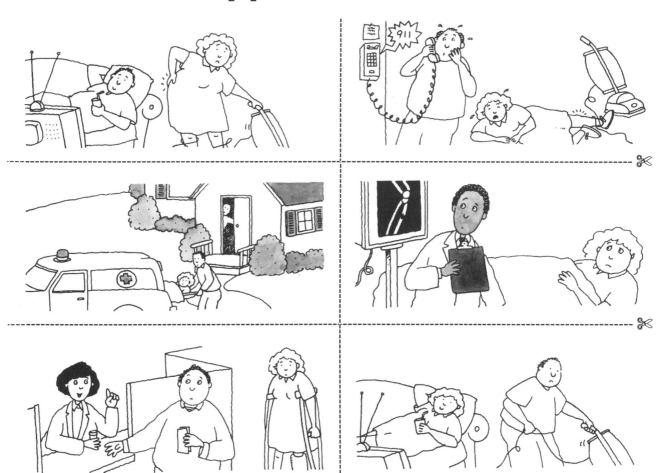

Bodybuilding (See Teacher's Notes, page 89.)

■ Listen to the directions.
■ Put a letter on the part of the body you hear mentioned.

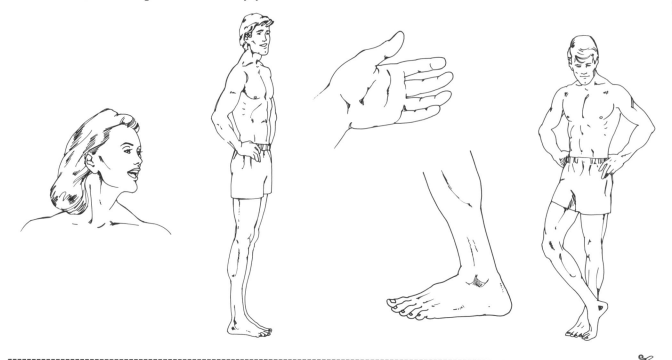

Is the Doctor In? (See Teacher's Notes, page 92.)

Drink hot tea with lemon, and don't talk so much!

Use a heating pad, get bed rest, and don't lift anything heavy!

Take two tablets every 4 hours and put an ice pack on your head.

You need a cast! Use some crutches to walk to the doctor's office.

Drink a little soda, lie down, and don't eat any more heavy food!

Use some ointment, don't go in the sun, and don't scratch!

Put some ice on your hand and next time be careful of the stove.

Wash your finger with soap and water and go get a Band-Aid.

Don't sneeze on me! You need some tissues and some soup.

Take Two Aspirin (See Teacher's Notes, page 90.)

- Look at the medicine labels below.
- Take turns asking your partner these kinds of questions:
    - Why do you take this medicine?
    - What is the dosage for this medicine?
    - When do you discard this medicine?
- Write in the missing information.
- When you don't hear an answer, ask "Could you repeat that?"

A

--✂

- Look at the medicine labels below.
- Take turns asking your partner these kinds of questions:
    - Why do you take this medicine?
    - What is the dosage for this medicine?
    - When do you discard this medicine?
- Write in the missing information.
- When you don't hear an answer, ask "Could you repeat that?"

B

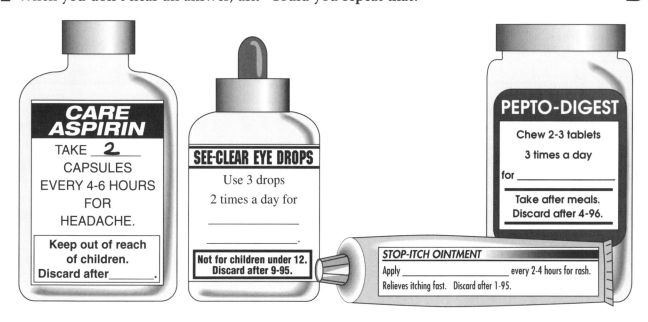

Health Fair (See Teacher's Notes, page 93.)

○ ○   ○ ○   ○ ○   ○ ○   ○ ○

HEALTH FAIR FORM

Registration
(Write the correct information here)

Mr. Mrs. Ms. _____   _____
              LAST NAME   BIRTHDATE

_____   _____   _____   _____
ADDRESS   CITY   STATE   ZIP

AILMENT: _____
         _____
         _____

DO NOT WRITE BELOW THIS LINE—FOR DOCTORS' USE ONLY

Height
(Stand next to chart. Stand up straight. Step away.)

_____ feet _____ inches

Weight
(Take off your shoes. Stand on scale. Step off.)

_____ pounds

Vision
(Cover one eye and read the chart.)

Left eye _____ /20   Right eye _____ /20

Pulse
(Run in place one minute. Stop. Find your pulse. Count the beats.)

_____ beats a minute

Reflexes
(Sit on the table. Relax.)

Right knee: ☐ excellent ☐ satisfactory ☐ unsatisfactory
Left knee: ☐ excellent ☐ satisfactory ☐ unsatisfactory

Interview
(Answer these questions.)

1. How many times a week do you eat fish?   ☐ 1-3 ☐ 4-6 ☐ 7+
2. How many times a week do you eat red meat?   ☐ 1-3 ☐ 4-6 ☐ 7+
3. How many times a week do you eat eggs?   ☐ 1-3 ☐ 4-6 ☐ 7+
4. How many times a week do you eat fruit?   ☐ 1-3 ☐ 4-6 ☐ 7+
5. How many hours do you sleep every night?   ☐ 3-4 ☐ 5-6 ☐ 7-8 ☐ 9+
6. Do you exercise?   ☐ Y ☐ N   How many days a week?   _____
7. Do you drink coffee?   ☐ Y ☐ N   How many cups a day?   _____
8. Do you smoke?   ☐ Y ☐ N   How many cigarettes a day? _____
9. Do you drink alcohol?   ☐ Y ☐ N   How often?   _____
10. Do you use salt?   ☐ Y ☐ N   How often?   _____

Living in the City
Teacher's Notes and Activity Sheets

Activity Title	■ Activity Type	Page
City Streets Students look at a city scene in the Dictionary and respond to a series of yes/no questions.	■ Silent Drill	100
A Library Tour Students listen to a librarian giving a tour of his library and point to the correct pictures in the Dictionary.	■ Listen and Point	101
Get Me That Eraser! Students listen to a teacher talking about things in her classroom and circle the correct item.	■ Listen and Circle	102
Some Schedule! Students listen to a student describing her day and sequence a series of pictures.	■ Listen and Sequence	103
Across From What? Students complete identical maps by asking for and giving the locations of different businesses.	■ Information Gap	104
Deliver the Letter "Office managers" tell "clerks" how to address four different envelopes.	■ TPR Pairs	105
Neighborhood Go Around Students move markers around a game board while answering questions and demonstrating knowledge about the places in the neighborhood.	■ Board Game	106
Bulletin Board City Students design and create three-dimensional buildings and write a description of their city.	■ Language Experience	107

Reproducible activity sheets on pages 109–112.

silent drill ■ whole class ■ 20 minutes

City Streets

Focus: Identifying common businesses and activities in a community.

Materials: Answer Cards and Don't Look Mask, p. 179; **The City, Dictionary, pp. 44–45.**

Before class, duplicate and cut apart a class set of the Answer Cards and two class sets of the Don't Look Mask. Look over the silent drill questions and the target vocabulary (step 4 below).

Preview

1. Hold up a set of answer cards and tell students that they will be listening to and answering a series of questions by raising the correct answer card.
2. Direct students to open their dictionaries to pages 44 and 45. Ask students to identify the places in The City, such as an office building, an apartment house, or a newsstand. Have students talk about the locations of the various buildings in relation to one another.

Presentation

3. Distribute the answer cards and two masks to each student. Have students cover the vocabulary at the bottom of pages 44 and 45 and listen to your questions about the pictures. Ask the first question: "Is the *pharmacy* across from the *post office?*" Tell students to raise the Yes card if the answer is yes, the No card if it is no, and the Not Sure card when there's not enough information to answer yes or no. Get class consensus on the first answer before continuing.

Practice (with Answers)

4. Ask the following questions:
   Is the *pharmacy* across from the *post office?* (Yes)
   Is there a *traffic light* on the corner? (Yes)
   Is there a *parking garage* next to the *fruit and vegetable market?* (No)
   Is there a *trash basket* in front of the *post office?* (No)
   Is there an *elevator* in the *office building?* (Not sure)
   Are the *department store* and the *bookstore* on the same street? (No)
   Is the *newsstand* next to the *subway station?* (Yes)
   Is there a *traffic cop* at the *bus stop?* (No)
   Are there *pedestrians* in the *crosswalk?* (Yes)
   Is there a *parking garage* in the area? (Yes)
   Are there *parking meters* in front of the *department store?* (Not sure)

Follow-up

5. Have students identify where various people are in the picture and what each person is doing.

Living in the City/Teacher's Notes ■ 100

A Library Tour

> **Focus:** Identifying items in a library.
>
> **Materials:** Don't Look Mask, p. 179; listening cassette; **The Public Library, Dictionary, p. 47.**
> ───────────
> Before class, duplicate a class set of the Don't Look Mask. Look over the target vocabulary in the tapescript below.

Preview

1. Tell students that they will be listening to a librarian talk about what you can see at his library.
2. Direct students to open their dictionaries to page 47. Write the following three categories on the board: Things you read, Things you use, People you talk to. Talk about the different kinds of reading material students see in the picture, and write the vocabulary on the board. Follow the same procedure for the other two categories.
3. Name an item from the first two categories and have students give you its color and/or location in the picture. Continue naming items until you've covered all the target vocabulary in the tapescript.

Presentation

4. Distribute the masks and have students cover the vocabulary at the bottom of the page. Tell students to listen to the tape and to point to the correct pictures in their dictionaries. Assure students that they will have several opportunities to hear the listening passage.
5. Play the tape through "She always has the information I need." Stop the tape and check to be sure that students are pointing to picture #23. Replay this section of the tape until all students are pointing to picture #23.

Practice

6. Play the tape, stopping when necessary. Replay the tape two to five times.

Follow-up

7. Check for comprehension of the target vocabulary by asking questions, such as "Where's the globe?" Students can respond by giving the location, saying "#19," or by pointing to the correct picture.

Variation

To make the follow-up more challenging, give students the floor plan of a local library. Have them label the sections and items in the library according to your directions. Then give students a list of items not on the floor plan (globe, photocopy machine, paperback rack) and have them go on a "scavenger hunt" to the local library to locate the items listed.

Tapescript (with Answers)

Listen to librarian Alex Apple giving a tour of his library. Point to the items or people you hear Alex talking about.

Welcome to the North Bend Library. I'm Alex Apple, the head librarian here, and I'm going to give you a tour of our wonderful public library. Let's start in the *reference section (21)*. I'm standing in front of the *reference librarian (23)*, Martha Burns. She always has the information I need.* Martha's desk is next to the *photocopy machine (18)*. Josh Adelson is making a copy right now. Josh loves to make copies.* In front of us you can see a table on the left. There's a *globe (19)* on the table. What a great way to look at the world! Do you see North and South America?* Find the book near the globe— the open one, not the closed one. That's an *atlas (20)*. You can use it to look at the world too!* Do you see a set of *shelves (26)* across from the table with the globe and atlas? The *dictionary (24)* is the large, open book on top. It's open to the letter K. Hmmm . . . kick, kind, king, kung fu. All the words on this page start with K.* Below the dictionary, on the first shelf, you can see our *encyclopedias (25)*. Those are the red books with the black letters. A is on the left and WXYZ is on the right. Great books, encyclopedias. You can get a lot of information from them.* Let's go to our *periodicals section (15)* now. That's where you see the *magazines (16)*. Can you find <u>Time</u> magazine on the rack?* There's a woman reading a journal at the table right near the magazines. And another woman is using the *microfilm reader (14)* near the *rows (11)* of books. Do you see her?* Our last stop of the day is at the *checkout desk (2)*. Our *library clerk (1)* is behind the checkout desk. She's holding a green book.* A woman is showing her a *library card (3)*. Do you see it in her hand? Library cards let you take our books home for two weeks, and library cards are free!* Behind the checkout desk you see the *card catalog (4)*. It's a big brown cabinet with many drawers. When you know the book you want, you can look for it in the card catalog. That concludes our tour for this morning. Come back soon for another visit. Happy reading!

Get Me That Eraser!

Focus: Identifying items in a classroom.

Materials: Activity sheet, p. 109; listening cassette; **A Classroom, Dictionary, p. 76.**

Before class, duplicate a class set of the activity sheet and look over the target vocabulary in the tapescript below.

Preview

1. Tell students that they will be listening to a teacher talking about different things in her classroom.
2. Have students open their dictionaries to page 76. Make open-ended statements about the target vocabulary and see if the class can guess which of the words you're talking about. "I have to write a note, I need a. . . ."; "When I write with chalk, I write on the. . . ."; "I teach students how to speak English. I'm a. . . ."

Presentation

3. Copy number 1 (the example) from the activity sheet onto the board. Explain the task to students, and assure them that they will have several opportunities to hear the listening passage.
4. Play the tape through number 1, ". . . I'm your math. . . ." Stop the tape and review the example on the board.
5. Distribute the activity sheets and review the directions.

Practice

6. Play the tape, stopping after each item. When necessary, replay each item two to five times.
7. Elicit students' responses for each item and get class consensus on the accuracy of the answers. Replay the tape to clarify any problems.

Follow-up

8. Write the following sets of words on the board:
   1) sharpener/eraser/paper 2) overhead projector/bulletin board/chalkboard 3) clock/bulletin board/teacher 4) loudspeaker/teacher/radio 5) chalk/pencil/pen. Divide students into groups of five and have students number off, 1–5, in their groups. Ask each group to decide together what each set of words has in common. When all the groups have finished, have the number 1s meet to compare their ideas about the first set of words, the number 2s meet to compare their ideas about the second set, and so on.

Tapescript (with Answers)

Listen to the teacher describe things in her classroom. Circle the correct words.

1. Hello, and welcome to room 7. I'm Ms. Martin and this semester I'm your math. . . . *(teacher)*
2. Jonathan, please come to the front of the class. Here's a piece of chalk. Now write this math problem on the. . . . *(chalkboard)*
3. Oh dear! Everything on the bulletin board keeps falling off. I have to get some more. . . . *(thumbtacks)*
4. We are going to learn about fractions today. Please open to page 79 in your. . . . *(textbooks)*
5. Lisa, may I have your attention please? It's not time to go home yet. Please stop watching the. . . . *(clock)*
6. Yes, Suntree? Oh, your pencil is broken? Look on my desk, you'll see the. . . . *(pencil sharpener)*
7. Excuse me everyone. Please stop talking, the principal is making an announcement. Everyone please listen to the. . . . *(loudspeaker)*
8. All right, that's the bell. Our class is dismissed. But remember, some other classes are still in session. Walk quietly in the. . . . *(hall)*

Some Schedule!

Focus: Identifying actions in a classroom.

Materials: Activity sheet, p. 109; listening cassette; **School Verbs, Dictionary, p. 77.**

Before class, duplicate a class set of the activity sheet and look over the target vocabulary in the tapescript below.

Preview

1. Tell students that they will be listening to an ESL student talk about her schedule and will number pictures in order.
2. Direct students to open their dictionaries to page 77. Invite volunteers to demonstrate various actions to the rest of the class in response to your instructions. Call out combinations, such as "Walk to the door and leave," or "Write your name on a piece of paper and read it out loud."

Presentation

3. Copy the first and the second pictures (the example) from the activity sheet onto the board. Explain the task to students, and assure them that they will have several opportunities to hear the listening passage.
4. Play the tape through number 1 ". . . from my apartment to the school," and review the example on the board.
5. Distribute the activity sheets and review the directions.

Practice

6. Play the tape, stopping after each item. When necessary, replay each item two to five times.
7. Elicit students' responses for each item and get consensus on the accuracy of the responses. Replay the tape to clarify any problems.

Follow-up

8. Have students compare their day to Sara's. Ask students to talk about how schools in their countries are the same or different.

Tapescript (with Answers)

Listen to Sara describe her day. Number the pictures as you hear the actions described.

1. My name's Sara Hernandez. I study ESL at the North Bend Learning Center. Every morning I *walk* to school. I like to walk, and it isn't too far from my apartment to the school. *(C)*
2. My first class is a listening lab. We *listen* to cassettes and practice pronunciation. My speaking's not too bad, but I need to practice my listening! *(B)*
3. My next class is a composition class. I *write* about all kinds of things in this class: my travels, my opinions, my life in the U.S. My teacher helps me to write what I want to say. *(G)*
4. At 10:00 I go to my typing class. I'm a very good typist in Spanish. Now I want to *type* well in English! *(E)*
5. My favorite class is after lunch: reading class. We *read* literature from all over the world, but of course, it's all in English. We even read a comic book last week! *(A)*
6. After reading I have a conversation class for an hour. I *talk* a lot in that class, but we all talk. The teacher likes a noisy class. *(H)*
7. At 4:00 I'm finished with my classes. I'm usually pretty tired at the end of the day. It feels good to *close* my books. *(F)*
8. It's hard work studying English. And I'm really happy when it's time to *leave* and walk back home. Of course, when I get home I have to cook, clean, do the laundry, and . . . You know, school's not so bad after all! *(D)*

Across From What?

Focus: Asking for and giving locations on a map.

Materials: Activity sheet, p. 110; manila folders (one per pair); **The City, Dictionary, pp. 44–45.**

Before class, duplicate half a class set of the activity sheet. Cut apart the A and B sections of the sheets and keep them separate. Copy the conversation from the activity sheet onto the board.

Preview

1. Tell students that they will be working in pairs to find out the location of the missing buildings on a map.
2. Direct students to look at pages 44 and 45 in their dictionaries. Ask students to tell you the locations of different buildings in the scene. Practice the following prepositions and prepositional phrases: across from, between, on the corner, around the corner from, and next to.

Presentation

3. Use the conversation on the board to model the language and clarification strategy you want students to use in the activity. Have the class practice the conversation, substituting different buildings.
4. Pair students and assign each one an A or a B role. Explain to students that they will each have a map with the names of different buildings missing. Point out that the missing buildings are on their partner's map. Tell students that they will take turns asking for and giving the location of the buildings in order to complete their maps.
5. Distribute a manila folder to each pair, to be propped up between the students as a screen. Distribute the A and B activity sheets to the appropriate partners. Review the directions and instruct students to look only at their own papers and not at their partner's.

6. Tell students to look at the example and to tell you where the bank is. Check comprehension by asking A students, "Where is the bakery?" Ask B students, "Where is the apartment building?"
7. Have one pair demonstrate the activity by asking for and giving the locations of buildings on their maps. Remind students to look only at their own maps.

Practice

8. Have students, in pairs, ask and answer questions about the missing buildings on their maps. Once they complete the task, partners can compare maps to be sure they are the same.

Follow-up

9. Have students draw maps of a major intersection near their school or homes, labeling as many buildings as they can. Students can use their maps as the basis for pair discussions about their neighborhoods: "Is there a post office in your area?" "Yes, it's across from the library, on Mission Street."

Deliver the Letter

> **Focus:** Giving and following directions for addressing an envelope.
>
> **Materials:** Activity sheet, p. 111; two 8-1/2" x 11" sheets of blank paper; manila folders (one per pair); two class sets of small envelopes; **The U.S. Postal System, Dictionary, p. 46.**
>
> ---
>
> *Before class, duplicate half a class set of the activity sheet. Cut apart envelopes 1, 2, 3, and 4 and keep them separate. Draw an enlarged version of envelope #1 on both of the 8-1/2" x 11" sheets of paper. Draw three large envelopes on the board and label them A, B, and C.*

Preview

1. Tell students that they will be addressing envelopes according to their partner's directions.
2. Direct students to open their dictionaries to page 46, and discuss the different envelopes on the page.
3. Have students tell you how to address envelope A on the board, using the return and mailing addresses pictured on the dictionary page (#8, #11). As students direct you ("Write K.L. Dobson in the upper left corner."), carry out their directions by writing the information in rectangle A on the board. Incorporate appropriate clarification questions as you respond to the directions, such as "What's the zip code?"; "What's the last name?"; "On the right or on the left?"
4. Invite a volunteer to address envelope B on the board, according to your directions. Be sure to modify the address from the one you wrote in step 3.

Presentation

5. Ask two of your more advanced students to come to the board. Call one student the "office manager" and the other the "clerk." Give the clerk a piece of chalk and the office manager one of the 8-1/2" x 11" pictures of envelope #1. Have the manager use the picture to tell the clerk how to address envelope C on the board. Show the other 8-1/2" x 11" envelope to the class so that the rest of the students know what the manager is looking at. Encourage the class to help the clerk and office manager complete their tasks.

Practice

6. Pair students and identify one as office manager, the other as clerk. Distribute a manila folder to each pair, to be propped up between the students as a screen. Explain that the office managers will give the information and the clerks will write what they hear on real envelopes. Stress that correct placement of the information is the goal of the activity.
7. Give envelope #1 to the managers and the small envelopes to the clerks. While pairs work on the first envelope, circulate and monitor their progress. When partners finish, they can compare envelopes and talk about any discrepancies.
8. After the pairs compare envelope #1, have them pick up envelope #2 and a blank envelope and repeat the activity. When partners finish #2, ask them to compare envelopes, switch roles, and pick up envelopes #3, #4, and two more blank envelopes.

Follow-up

9. Give each partner in the pair another blank envelope and have partners exchange addresses. Have students write their own return addresses and their partner's mailing address on the envelope. Later, students can use the envelopes to send notes or greeting cards to their partners.

Neighborhood Go Around

Focus: Demonstrating knowledge of places in the neighborhood.

Materials: Activity sheet, p. 112; Picture Cards #87–#100, p. 184; coins; scratch paper; four 8-1/2" x 11" sheets of blank paper; clips or small envelopes; **The City, Dictionary, pp. 44–45.**

Before class, duplicate the activity sheet (one per four students). Duplicate the picture cards (one set per four students). Cut apart the picture cards and clip them together in sets. Draw the following pictures on the 8-1/2" x 11" sheets of paper (one picture per sheet): a bank, a park, an apartment building, and a school.

Preview

1. Tell students that they are going to test their knowledge of places in the neighborhood by playing a board game with their classmates.
2. Direct students to open their dictionaries to pages 44 and 45. Write the following statements and questions on the board: "Say it and spell it," "Is there one in your neighborhood?"; "What can you do here?"; and "Who can you see here?" Ask the class to choose a building from pages 44 and 45, and to respond to each statement or question on the board.

Presentation

3. Copy the activity sheet onto the board, filling in only the first four squares. Put the 8-1/2" x 11" places picture cards on the chalk ledge, face down. Invite three volunteers to the front of the room. Have the volunteers write their names on separate pieces of scratch paper while you do the same. Tape the papers to the "Start" square. Explain that the papers are the game markers.
4. Show the class a coin and demonstrate flipping it "heads" and "tails." Flip the coin and move your marker on the board, one

space for heads, two spaces for tails. Move your marker to the square "Pick a card: Say it and spell it" or "Say your address." Have the class read the directions aloud. Follow the directions. Play two rounds of the game with the three volunteers. Get class consensus on the accuracy of the volunteers' responses. Point out that when a response is not correct, the player cannot flip the coin on her next turn and must answer the same question again.

Practice

5. Divide the class into groups of four. Distribute the activity sheets (game boards), picture card sets, coins, and scratch paper to each group. Have each group create four "markers" and place them on the "Start" square.
6. Check for general understanding of the game by asking yes/no questions, such as "Do I move two spaces for heads?" and "Do I pick a card from the top of the pile?"
7. Set a 20-minute time limit for the game and begin play.
8. Circulate and monitor student practice. (In cases where groups cannot come to consensus, you serve as referee.)

Follow-up

9. Divide the class into two teams, A and B. Copy the activity sheet onto the board, replacing the directions with numbers. Have team members take turns flipping coins and answering your questions (the original questions or new ones).

Variation

Divide the class into groups of five. Students 1 and 2 form team A, students 3 and 4 form team B, and student 5 serves as the referee. Proceed as before (step 9). Allow referees to use the dictionary and other resources to decide if spelling and other responses are accurate.

Bulletin Board City

Focus: Identifying common buildings and describing a city.

Materials: Construction paper; butcher paper; half a class set each of scissors, glue sticks or tape, and colored markers or pencils; **The City, Dictionary, pp. 44–45.**

Before class, estimate the number of buildings your students will create and cover a sufficient amount of bulletin board space with butcher paper. Gather together the drawing materials, scissors, and glue sticks or tape dispensers. Make a sample building out of a piece of construction paper. Draw windows and a door on your "building" and label it "(Your Name)'s Apartments."

Preview

1. Tell students that they will be working as a class to create different buildings to design a city, and to write a description of their neighborhood for a travel guide.
2. Draw two intersecting lines (streets) on the board and ask students to label the streets for you. Draw a square on the north side of the east-west street and label the square "park." Show the class your sample building and have students tell you where to place it on the board in relation to the intersection and the park. Next, demonstrate how you created the building. Have students follow along, using their notebook paper, as you refold the building. Demonstrate different ways to decorate the building, such as cutting out the shape of the roof, and cutting and pasting windows, signs, and doors on the building.

Presentation

3. Elicit the names of buildings and places in the city. List these places on the board until you have as many places as you have students.

4. Have each student choose one building while you distribute the materials to the class. (If students do not get the color markers or construction paper they prefer, they can negotiate with other students for the materials they'd like.)

Practice

5. Give students 20 minutes to create their buildings. Circulate and talk to the students while they are working on their buildings.
6. After 20 minutes, have those students who have completed their buildings come to the board and tape their buildings wherever they'd like. Assign two students who have completed the activity the role of city planners. Their job is to facilitate the placement of the buildings on the board. Ask the other students to create additional elements, such as cars, buses, people, and trees.

Follow-up

7. Tell students that their buildings are in one city. Elicit a description of this city from the class by asking questions, such as "What's this city's name?"; "What kind of city is this?"; "What can you do in this city?"; "Are there any...?"; "Is there a...?"; "What's missing in the city?"; and "What's the best thing about this city?" Write the description on the board exactly as the students tell it to you. Have students read the description aloud and copy it.

   The following is a typical level-one story: This is Lucky City. It is beautiful city. There are many buildings here. You can see a movie in the theater. There's no gas station, electric cars. This the best city for playing soccer, there is big park.

Your Notes

Get Me That Eraser! (See Teacher's Notes, page 102.)

■ Listen to the teacher describe things in her classroom.
■ Circle the correct word.

1. (teacher)	computer	pencil
2. textbook	chalkboard	clock
3. students	thumbtacks	pencils
4. hall	chalkboard	textbooks
5. clock	teacher	loudspeaker
6. textbook	chalk	pencil sharpener
7. pencil	loudspeaker	bulletin board
8. hall	students	clock

-- ✂

Some Schedule! (See Teacher's Notes, page 103.)

■ Listen to Sara describe her day.
■ Number the pictures as you hear the actions described.

Across From What? <small>(See Teacher's Notes, page 104.)</small>

- Look at your map.
- Ask and answer questions about these places:
  park, drugstore, parking garage, apartment building.
- Write in the missing places on your map.
- Use this conversation as a model:
  Where's the bank?
    It's across from the bookstore.
  It's across from what?
    The bookstore.

A

| 2nd AVENUE | _____ | BOOKSTORE | LIBRARY | _____ | MARKET | SHOE STORE | _____ | 3rd AVENUE |

MAIN STREET

| 2nd AVENUE | SCHOOL | BANK | BAKERY | _____ | OFFICE BUILDING | DEPARTMENT STORE | NEWSSTAND | 3rd AVENUE |

--- ✂

- Look at your map.
- Ask and answer questions about these buildings:
  library, market, office building, newsstand.
- Write in the missing buildings on your map.
- Use this conversation as a model.
  Where's the bank?
    It's across from the bookstore.
  It's across from what?
    The bookstore.

B

| 2nd AVENUE | PARK | BOOKSTORE | _____ | DRUGSTORE | _____ | SHOE STORE | APARTMENT BUILDING | 3rd AVENUE |

MAIN STREET

| 2nd AVENUE | SCHOOL | BANK | BAKERY | PARKING GARAGE | _____ | DEPARTMENT STORE | _____ | 3rd AVENUE |

Deliver the Letter (See Teacher's Notes, page 105.)

--- ✂

#1

Martin Smith
1737 Pine Avenue, Apt. #4
Van Nuys, CA 91406

USA

Mr. B. Clinton
1700 Pennsylvania Avenue
Washington, DC 20500

--- ✂

#2

Jane Jackson
1839 Madison Avenue, #1208
NY, NY 10016

USA

IRS
111 Constitution Avenue, NW
Washington, DC 20500

--- ✂

#3

Neko Lehrburger
3458 Bee Lane
Austin, TX 78759

USA

FBI
1900 Half Street, SW
Washington, DC 20500

--- ✂

#4

Mrs. Norman Maine
619 18th Avenue
Coos Bay, OR 97420

USA

Social Security Administration
801 N. Randolph Street
Washington, DC 20500

--- ✂

Neighborhood Go Around (See Teacher's Notes, page 106.)

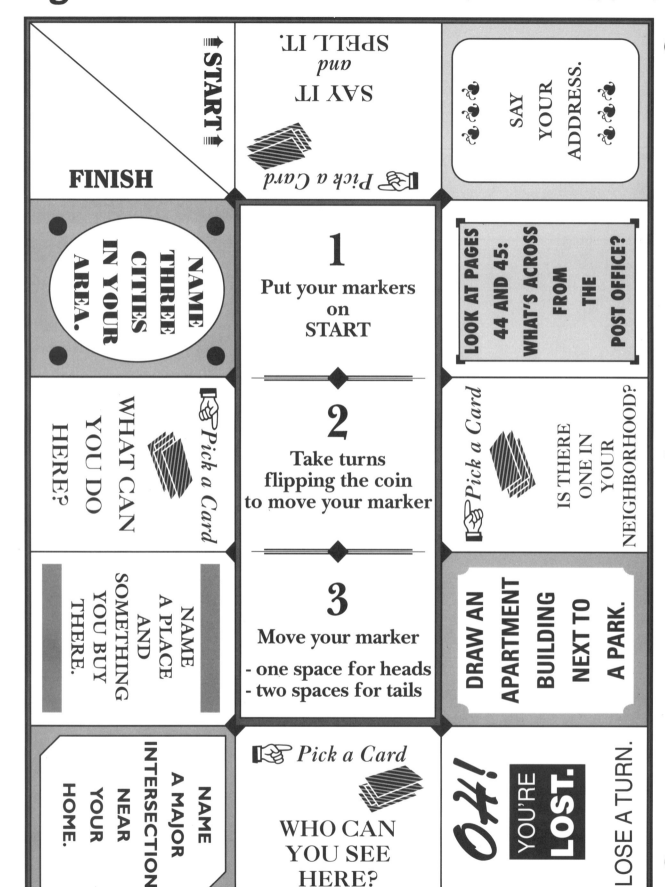

START

SAY IT *and* SPELL IT.

Pick a Card

SAY YOUR ADDRESS.

FINISH

NAME THREE CITIES IN YOUR AREA.

1 Put your markers on START

LOOK AT PAGES 44 AND 45: WHAT'S ACROSS FROM THE POST OFFICE?

Pick a Card

WHAT CAN YOU DO HERE?

2 Take turns flipping the coin to move your marker

Pick a Card

IS THERE ONE IN YOUR NEIGHBORHOOD?

NAME A PLACE AND SOMETHING YOU BUY THERE.

3 Move your marker
- one space for heads
- two spaces for tails

DRAW AN APARTMENT BUILDING NEXT TO A PARK.

NAME A MAJOR INTERSECTION NEAR YOUR HOME.

Pick a Card

WHO CAN YOU SEE HERE?

Oh! YOU'RE LOST. LOSE A TURN.

Getting Places
Teacher's Notes and Activity Sheets

Reproducible activity sheets on pages 123–126.

Flight 401 to Pittsburgh

> **Focus:** Identifying items in an airport.
>
> **Materials:** Answer Cards and Don't Look Mask, p. 179; **Air Travel, Dictionary, p. 56.**
>
> ___
>
> *Before class, duplicate and cut apart a class set of the Answer Cards and Don't Look Mask. Look over the silent drill questions and the target vocabulary (step 4 below).*

Preview

1. Hold up a set of answer cards and tell students that they will be listening to and answering a series of questions by raising the correct answer card.
2. Direct students to open their dictionaries to page 56. Ask students to imagine that they are travelers at the airport and to talk about what they are doing.

Presentation

3. Distribute the answer cards and the masks. Have students cover the vocabulary at the bottom of the page and listen to your questions about the pictures. Ask the first question: "Is the *porter* holding a *dolly?*" Tell students to raise the Yes card if the answer is yes, the No card if it is no, and the Not Sure card when there's not enough information to answer yes or no. Get class consensus on the first answer before continuing.

Practice (with Answers)

4. Ask the following questions:
   Is the *porter* holding a *dolly?* (Yes)
   Is the woman at the check-in counter holding a *ticket?* (No)
   Is the woman's *garment bag* heavy? (Not Sure)
   Is a child walking through the *metal detector?* (No)
   Is the *conveyor belt* moving? (Not Sure)
   Is there a *security guard* in the cockpit? (No)
   Is the *boarding pass* for the non-smoking section? (Yes)
   Is the *pilot* standing in the *aisle?* (No)
   Is the *flight attendant* putting coffee on the *tray table?* (No)
   Is the *luggage compartment* open? (Yes)

Follow-up

5. Have students talk about the conversations that might be taking place. Ask students to identify the people and what each person is saying.

Mike's Auto Repair

> **Focus:** Identifying parts of a car.
>
> **Materials:** Don't Look Mask, p. 179; listening cassette; **Cars, Dictionary, pp. 50–51.**
>
> *Before class, duplicate a set of the Don't Look Mask. Look over the target vocabulary in the tapescript below.*

Preview

1. Tell students that they will be listening to the owner of an auto repair shop tell his employee the jobs that need to be done.
2. Direct students to open their dictionaries to pages 50 and 51. Ask students to identify the parts of a car that break down or need to be checked most often. List students' suggestions on the board and add any target vocabulary that is missing.

Presentation

3. Distribute the masks and have students cover the vocabulary at the bottom of the page. Tell students to listen to the tape and to point to the car parts mentioned. Assure students that they will have several opportunities to hear the listening passage.
4. Play the tape through ". . . he almost got a speeding ticket last week, so check the *speedometer.*" Stop the tape and check to be sure that students are pointing to picture #10. Replay this section of the tape until all students are pointing to picture #10.

Practice

5. Play the tape, stopping when necessary. Replay the tape two to five times.

Follow-up

6. Check for comprehension of the target vocabulary by asking questions, such as "What part of the car tells you how fast the car is traveling?" Students can respond by saying the number or the word.

Variation

To make this activity more challenging, after playing the tape, have students, in pairs, write a dialogue in which they describe to Mike different car problems and offer Mike's suggestions. Have students practice and present their dialogues to the class.

Tapescript (with Answers)

Listen while Mike tells his new employee, Leon, about the car repairs they have to do. Point to the parts of a car you hear Mike talking about.

Well, Leon, we've got a lot of cars to fix this morning. Let's get to work. Look at the inside of this car. The owner said he almost got a speeding ticket last week, so check the *speedometer (10).** And the *steering wheel (8)* is loose. Tighten it, okay?* He also said the lock on the *glove compartment (20)* is broken. His little boy stuck a pencil in it.* On the outside, check the *windshield wipers (6).* It's probably going to rain soon.* Next we have to work on the white station wagon. The *license plate (28)* looks like it's about to fall off. You can get a ticket for that, you know.* Also the *brake light (29)* is out too, so change that. The brake light is the red one, Leon.* Oh, I didn't notice this. See the right rear *tire (37)?* It's flat. Put some air in it.* The blue sedan over here has a *spare tire (39).* Check it and make sure it's not flat.* On this car it's kept in the *trunk (40).* See, I already opened it for you. Boy, that trunk sure looks clean, doesn't it.* After you do that, take care of the yellow *hatchback (43).** The *sunroof (44)* has problems. You know how those things always leak.* And the *front bumper (51)* is bent near the license plate. Maybe you can straighten it, okay? I like the way bumpers have that black rubber in them, don't you?* Now look at the *engine (F)* of this one. Looks great, doesn't it?* Well, check the *radiator (56).* It probably needs water. That's the thing in the front, Leon.* The *battery (54)* needs water too. It's on the left.* Maybe you can take out the *dipstick (58)* right now, and check the oil. I see you're already doing it! Watch your hand.* Be very, very careful with this baby, Leon. You wouldn't want to mess up the boss's new car, would you?

Highway Rollers

Focus: Identifying types of trucks.

Materials: Activity sheet, p. 123; listening cassette; **Trucks, Dictionary, p. 49.**

Before class, duplicate a class set of the activity sheet and copy the first item from the activity sheet onto the board: fuel truck, tow truck, lunch truck. Look over the target vocabulary in the tapescript below.

Preview

1. Tell students that they will be listening to people talk about their jobs and the kinds of trucks they need.
2. Direct students to open their dictionaries to page 49. Point to the words on the board and have students find them on the dictionary page. Make open-ended statements, such as "The battery in the car is dead. I need to call a. . . ."; "I forgot my sandwich again! Well, I guess I'll have to buy one at the. . . ."; and "My apartment is really cold. Everyone is waiting for the. . . ." Elicit answers from the class.

Presentation

3. Have students look at number 1 (the example) on the board. Explain the task to students, and assure them that they will have several opportunities to hear the listening passage.
4. Play the tape through number 1, "We need you to drive the. . . ." Stop the tape and review the example on the board.
5. Distribute the activity sheets and review the directions.

Practice

6. Play the tape, stopping after each item. When necessary, replay each item two to five times.

7. Elicit students' responses for each item and get class consensus on the accuracy of the answers. Replay the tape to clarify any problems.

Follow-up

8. Write these two categories on the board: Transport and Maintenance. Have students use the dictionary page to brainstorm the names of trucks used to transport or deliver and trucks used to maintain or clean. Ask students to name several items that could be carried in each truck, and have volunteers write their ideas on the board.

Tapescript (with Answers)

Listen to the people talk about different jobs. Circle the kind of truck needed for each job.

1. Frank, there's an accident out on Highway 101. No one was hurt but we have to clear those cars off the road. We need you to drive the. . . ." *(tow truck)*
2. Hello, Barbara? Can you help me with a job at Food Fair supermarkets? [pause] No, not tomatoes. We've got 4000 pounds of potatoes in that. . . ." *(tractor trailer)*
3. The county is building a new playground and they need two tons of clean sand. My partner, George McKenna, and I will be driving a. . . ." *(dump truck)*
4. Hello, is this Sergei's Catering? [pause] Good, 'cus I got 40 hungry guys over at the Vineland construction site. [pause] Whaddaya mean, you're running late? Just hurry up and get the. . . ." *(lunch truck)*
5. Dan Wolenski just found a part-time job delivering magazines. His company will pay for the gas, but Dan needs a clean driving record and his own . . . ." *(pickup truck)*
6. Hello, José David? We need you for a one-week job with Coastal Transport. [pause] Yeah, some family is moving from a big house—furniture, refrigerator, that kind of stuff. Big job. They're moving from California to New York. [pause] Whaddaya mean you have a bad back? All you gotta do is drive a. . . ." *(moving van)*
7. Ali has a good job working for the city. He keeps our roads nice and clean. Every morning he has to make sure the big broom in the front is working before he takes out the. . . ." *(street cleaner)*
8. Kim and Tony are replacing the regular sanitation crew. Kim will drive while Tony empties out all the trash cans. Tony has to wear gloves and be very careful throwin' that trash in the back of the. . . ." *(garbage truck)*

All Aboard!

Preview

1. Tell students that they will be listening to people talking about different kinds of transportation.
2. Direct students to open their dictionaries to pages 54, 55, and 56. Ask students to identify the different kinds of transportation pictured on the pages: bus, subway, train, taxi, airplane. Discuss the vocabulary listed under each kind. Point out that much of the vocabulary for subways and trains (conductor, track, platform, and station) is the same.

Presentation

3. Copy number 1 (the example) from the activity sheet onto the board. Explain the task to students, and assure them that they will have several opportunities to hear the listening passage.
4. Play the tape through number 1, "Please stand away from the *platform*." Stop the tape and review the example on the board.
5. Distribute the activity sheets and review the directions.

Practice

6. Play the tape, stopping after each item. When necessary, replay each item two to five times.
7. Elicit student responses for each number and get class consensus on the accuracy of the answers. Replay the tape to clarify problems.

Follow-up

8. Have students, in pairs, role play being passengers and drivers or conductors on one of the vehicles, such as a bus, a train, or a subway. Ask volunteers to share their conversations.

Tapescript (with Answers)

Listen to the people talking. Check the correct form of transportation.

1. Arriving on track 8, the commuter *train* from Albany. Please stand away from the platform. *(train/subway)*
2. Honey, I forgot to ask the bus driver for our *transfer*. Please get it. *(bus)*
3. Okay, sir, the *fare* is $16.50. I'll make out your *receipt* in a minute. *(taxi)*
4. Ladies and gentlemen, please be sure your *carry-on bags* are in the *luggage compartment* and your *tray tables* are in the upright position. Take-off will be in approximately five minutes. *(airplane)*
5. Let's see. The *meter* said $8.50, plus $1.50 for a *tip*. Martin, give the *cab driver* a ten. *(taxi)*
6. Pull the *cord*, Fred. That's our stop. We get off at Broadway. *(bus)*
7. Please show your *boarding pass* to the flight attendant before entering the *cabin*. You're in the non-smoking section, miss. *(airplane)*
8. Okay, Maxie. You want to see all the instruments? Let's ask the *pilot* if you can go into the *cockpit*. *(airplane)*
9. Here's your *token*, Enrico. Put it in the slot and go through the *turnstile*. Let's hurry. I see our subway coming. *(train/subway)*
10. Gee, Fred, this is going to be a great game tonight. I'll meet you at the station at 4 o'clock. Wait for me by the *ticket window*, OK? *(train/subway)*

Frequent Flyers

> **Focus:** Asking for and giving information on boarding passes.
>
> **Materials:** Activity sheet, page 124; manila folders (one per pair); **Air Travel, Dictionary, p. 56.**
>
> ---
>
> *Before class, duplicate half a class set of the activity sheet. Cut apart the A and B sections of the sheets and keep them separate. Copy the questions from the activity sheet onto the board and draw a boarding pass with the following headings, but no information: Gate, Seat, Smoking/ Non-Smoking, Date, Destination, and Departure Time.*

Preview

1. Tell students that they will be working in pairs to find out the missing information on boarding passes.
2. Direct students to open their dictionaries to page 56 and to locate the boarding pass (#18). Have students tell you how to fill in the boarding pass on the board using the information on page 56. Demonstrate how to clarify information by repeating it: "Seat 10A?" or "November 3?"

Presentation

3. Use the questions on the board to model the language and clarification strategy you want students to use in the activity. Have the class practice asking and answering the questions using the boarding pass.
4. Pair students and assign each one an A or a B role. Explain to students that they will each have boarding passes with some information missing. Point out that the missing information is on their partner's boarding pass. Tell students that they will take turns asking for and giving this missing information in order to complete their passes.

5. Distribute a manila folder to each pair, to be propped up between the students as a screen. Distribute the A and B activity sheets to the appropriate partners. Review the directions and instruct students to look only at their own papers and not at their partner's.
6. Tell students to look at the boarding pass for Flight 33 and tell you the seat number. Check comprehension by asking A students, "What is the departure time for Flight 33?" Ask B students, "What is the destination for Flight 33?"
7. Have one pair demonstrate the activity by asking for and giving information about Flight 33. Remind students to look only at their own boarding passes.

Practice

8. Have students, in pairs, ask and answer questions about the missing information on their boarding passes. Once they complete the task, partners can compare boarding passes to be sure they are the same.

Follow-up

9. Tell the class that they are going to "take a vacation." Have pairs form groups of four. Have each group agree on a destination, a time of departure, and preferred seat assignments. Then have the groups create a boarding pass for their flight, and present their travel plans to the class.

You Be the Witness

Focus: Describing positions and positioning vehicles on a highway.

Materials: Activity sheet, p. 125; two 8-1/2" x 11" blank sheets of paper; manila folders (one per pair); six 4" x 6" index cards; paper clips; scratch paper; tape; **Highway Travel, Dictionary, p. 53.**

Before class, duplicate half a class set of the activity sheet. Cut apart highways #1–#4, and the vehicle cards. Keep the highways separate and clip together sets of the vehicle cards. Draw an enlarged version of highway #1 on both 8-1/2" x 11" sheets of paper. Copy the six vehicles from the activity sheet onto the 4" x 6" index cards (one vehicle per card). Draw three vertical lines for lanes on the board, each lane wide enough to accommodate the index cards.

Preview

1. Tell students that they will be placing cars on a highway scene according to their partner's directions.
2. Direct students to open their dictionaries to page 53. Tell students that a few minutes after this picture was taken an accident occurred on the northbound side of the highway (the right side of the highway). Play the part of a police officer asking witnesses to describe the scene before the accident happened. Use questions, such as "Where was the bus?" or "Was it in the center lane?"
3. Have students tell you how to recreate the highway scene (northbound side) on page 53 in the dictionary. Draw a compass on the board to orient students to the direction of traffic. As students direct you ("Put the bus in the center lane."), carry out their directions by taping the vehicle index cards to the lanes on the board. Incorporate appropriate clarification questions as you respond to the directions, such as "Which

lane?" and "In front of the bus or behind?"
4. Invite a volunteer to the board to recreate a highway scene according to your directions. Modify the scene from the one used in step 3.

Presentation

5. Ask two of your more advanced students to come to the board. Call one student the "witness" and the other the "police officer." Give the officer the 4" x 6" vehicle cards and the witness one of the 8-1/2" x 11" pictures of highway #1. Have the witness use the picture to tell the officer how to recreate the highway scene. Show the class the other 8-1/2" x 11" highway so that students know what the witness is looking at. Encourage the class to help the witness and officer complete their tasks.

Practice

6. Pair students and identify one as a witness, the other as a police officer. Distribute a manila folder to each pair, to be propped up between the students as a screen. Explain that the witnesses will describe the scene and the officers will place the vehicles on the highway according to what they hear.
7. Give highway #1 to the witnesses and the scratch paper and vehicle cards to the officers. Have the officers draw three lanes on their paper. While pairs work on highway #1, circulate and monitor their progress. When partners have completed highway #1, they can compare pictures and discuss any discrepancies.
8. After pairs finish comparing highway #1, have them pick up highway #2 and repeat the activity. When partners finish #2, ask them to compare pictures, switch roles, pick up highways #3 and #4, and exchange the scratch paper and vehicle pictures.

Follow-up

9. Have students talk about the different reasons for car accidents, such as following too closely, running red lights, or drinking while driving.

Transportation Go Around

Focus: Demonstrating knowledge about transportation.

Materials: Activity sheet, p. 126; Vehicle Pictures, p. 126; coins; scratch paper; four 8-1/2″ x 11″ sheets of blank paper; clips; **Highway Travel, Public Transportation,** and **Air Travel, Dictionary, pp. 53–56.**

Before class, duplicate the activity sheet (one per four students). Cut apart the vehicle pictures at the bottom of the activity sheet and clip them together in sets. Draw the following pictures on the 8-1/2″ x 11″ sheets of paper (one picture per sheet): a van, an airplane, a bus, a truck.

Preview

1. Tell students that they are going to test their knowledge of transportation by playing a board game with their classmates.
2. Direct students to open their dictionaries to page 53. Write the following statements and questions on the board: "Say it and spell it," "Tell how you're traveling," "Can you operate this vehicle?"; and "Name one part of this vehicle." Ask the class to choose a form of transportation from page 53 and to respond to each statement or question on the board. For additional practice, repeat the procedure using pages 54 and 55.

Presentation

3. Copy the activity sheet onto the board, filling in only the first four squares. Put the 8-1/2″ x 11″ pictures on the chalk ledge, face down. Invite three volunteers to the front of the room. Have the volunteers write their names on separate pieces of scratch paper while you do the same. Tape the papers to the "Start" square. Explain that the papers are the game markers.

4. Show the class a coin and demonstrate flipping it "heads" and "tails." Flip the coin and move your marker on the board: one space for heads, two spaces for tails. Move your marker to the square "Pick a card: Say it and spell it," or "Name something you see at an airport." Have the class read the directions aloud. Follow the directions. Play two rounds of the game with the three volunteers. Get class consensus on the accuracy of the volunteers' responses. Point out that when a response is not correct, the player cannot flip the coin on his next turn and must answer the same question again.

Practice

5. Divide the class into groups of four. Distribute the activity sheets (game boards), sets of pictures, coins, and scratch paper to each group. Have each group create four "markers" and place them on the "Start" square.
6. Check for general understanding of the game by asking yes/no questions, such as "Do I move two spaces for heads?" and "Do I pick a card from the top of the pile?"
7. Set a 20-minute time limit for the game and begin play.
8. Circulate and monitor student practice. (In cases where groups cannot come to consensus, you serve as referee.)

Follow-up

9. Divide the class into two teams, A and B. Copy the activity sheet onto the board, replacing the directions with numbers. Have team members take turns flipping coins and answering your questions (the original questions or new ones).

Variation

Divide the class into groups of five. Students 1 and 2 form team A, students 3 and 4 form team B, and student 5 serves as the referee. Proceed as before (step 9). Allow referees to use the dictionary and other resources to decide if spelling and other responses are accurate.

Going My Way?

Focus: Asking for and giving information about travel plans.

Materials: Activity sheet, p. 125; four 8-1/2" x 11" blank sheets of paper; **The United States of America, Dictionary, pp. 72–73.**

Before class, duplicate two copies of the activity sheet. You will need a matching set of cue slips for every two students. (If you have more than 32 students, duplicate three copies of the sheet.) Cut apart the cue slips and mix them up. Copy the following phrases onto the four 8-1/2" x 11" sheets of paper (one phrase per sheet): "Madison, Wisconsin—Bus" (two), "Madison, Wisconsin—Car," and "St. Louis, Missouri—Bus."

Preview

1. Tell students that they are going to be tourists traveling across the United States. To make their journey, they will need to find a classmate going to the same destination by the same mode of transportation.
2. Direct students to open their dictionaries to pages 72 and 73. Together, look at the map and have students tell you the states they've visited or would like to visit. Ask about the different kinds of transportation used to get to those places, and list the names on the board.

Presentation

3. Copy the following conversation onto the board: Student 1: "I'm going to Madison, Wisconsin. Where are you going?" Student 2: "I'm going to Madison, too." Student 1: "How are you going?" Student 2: "By car, and you?" Student 1: "By bus." Model the conversation for the class. Then have the class practice, substituting other destinations and modes of transportation.

4. Invite four volunteers to the front of the room and give each one an 8-1/2" x 11" cue slip. Have the volunteers tell the class where they are going and how they are getting there, using the cue slips to model the conversation. When one student finds another student with an identical cue slip, have the two students stand together. Point out that all students will find a partner during the activity.
5. Look at the U.S. map and ask students what states they would need to travel through to get from their present state to Madison, Wisconsin.

Practice

6. Randomly distribute the cue slips and have students circulate looking for someone with the same destination and mode of transportation. When students find their match, have them sit together to decide on their route by making a list of the states they'll have to travel through. Circulate and monitor student practice.

Follow-up

7. After the mixer, have partners share with the class their various destinations and the states they'll be traveling through. Have the class reach consensus on whether or not the routes chosen are correct.

Variations

To make the activity easier, before beginning the mixer, review all the destinations with the class.

To make the activity more challenging, have students go to an atlas and determine the total mileage for their trip and the major cities through which they will travel.

Your Notes

Highway Rollers (See Teacher's Notes, page 116.)

- Listen to the people talk about different jobs.
- Circle the kind of truck needed for each job.

1. fuel truck   (tow truck)   lunch truck

2. tractor trailer   street cleaner   snow plow

3. garbage truck   snow plow   dump truck

4. cement truck   lunch truck   panel truck

5. pickup truck   transporter   fuel truck

6. flatbed   tow truck   moving van

7. dump truck   tractor trailer   street cleaner

8. garbage truck   fuel truck   panel truck

All Aboard! (See Teacher's Notes, page 117.)

- Listen to the people talking.
- Check (√) the kind of transportation.

	BUS	TAXI	TRAIN/SUBWAY	AIRPLANE
1			√	
2				
3				
4				
5				
6				
7				
8				
9				
10				

Frequent Flyers (See Teacher's Notes, page 118.)

■ Look at the boarding passes below.
■ Take turns asking your partner these kinds of questions:
    What's the destination for Flight 33?
    What's the departure time for Flight 33?
    What's the gate number for Flight 33?
    What's the seat number for Flight 33?
■ Write in the missing information.
■ When you don't hear an answer, ask "Would you say that again?"

A

- ✂

■ Look at the boarding passes below.
■ Take turns asking your partner these kinds of questions:
    What's the destination for Flight 33?
    What's the departure time for Flight 33?
    What's the gate number for Flight 33?
    What's the seat number for Flight 33?
■ Write in the missing information.
■ When you don't hear an answer, ask "Would you say that again?"

B

Going My Way? (See Teacher's Notes, page 121.)

Madison, Wisconsin—Bus	Denver, Colorado—Bus
Las Vegas, Nevada—Bus	St. Louis, Missouri—Train
Wichita, Kansas—Train	Bangor, Maine—Car
Denver, Colorado—Car	St. Louis, Missouri—Car
Cedar Rapids, Iowa—Car	Portland, Oregon—Car
Madison, Wisconsin—Car	Denver, Colorado—Train
Las Vegas, Nevada—Car	St. Louis, Missouri—Bus
Wichita, Kansas—Bus	Bangor, Maine—Train

You Be the Witness (See Teacher's Notes, page 119.)

Transportation Go Around (See Teacher's Notes, page 120.)

START / FINISH

Pick a Card — SAY IT AND SPELL IT.

NAME SOMETHING YOU SEE AT AN AIRPORT.

Pick a Card — TELL HOW YOU ARE TRAVELING.

NAME A TRANSPORTATION JOB.

1 PUT YOUR MARKERS ON **START**

2 TAKE TURNS FLIPPING THE COIN TO MOVE YOUR MARKER

3 MOVE YOUR MARKER
- ONE SPACE FOR HEADS
- TWO SPACES FOR TAILS

NAME SOMETHING THAT COMES TO THE STORE BY TRUCK.

THE BUS IS LATE. LOSE A TURN.

Pick a Card — NAME ONE PART OF THIS VEHICLE.

DESCRIBE ONE VEHICLE ON THIS PAGE.

LOOK AT PAGE 53.

Pick a Card — CAN YOU OPERATE THIS VEHICLE?

NAME A PLACE YOU WANT TO VISIT.

NAME SOMETHING YOU SEE ON THE HIGHWAY.

Talking About Jobs
Teacher's Notes and Activity Sheets

Reproducible activity sheets on pages 137–140.

Who am I? What am I Doing?

Focus: Identifying occupations.

Materials: Answer Cards and Don't Look Mask, p. 179; 12 3″ x 5″ index cards; **Occupations III, Dictionary, p. 86.**

Before class, duplicate and cut apart a class set of the Answer Cards and Don't Look Mask. Copy the vocabulary from section A of Dictionary page 86 on the index cards. (One occupation per card.) Look over the silent drill questions and the target vocabulary (step 4) below.

Preview

1. Hold up a set of answer cards and tell students that they will be listening to and answering a series of questions by raising the correct answer card.
2. Direct students to open their dictionaries to page 86 and to look at picture A (Media and Arts). Ask students to identify the people working in the pictures. Talk about what each person is doing and what tools he or she is using.

Presentation

3. Distribute the answer cards and masks. Have students cover pictures B and C and the vocabulary at the bottom of the page. Tell students to listen to your questions about the occupations depicted. Ask the first question: "Look at the weather forecaster. Is he standing?" Tell your students to raise the Yes card if the answer is yes, the No card if it is no, and the Not Sure card when there's not enough information to answer yes or no. Get class consensus on the first answer before continuing.

Practice (with Answers)

4. Ask the following questions:
   Look at the *weather forecaster*. Is he standing? (Yes)
   Find the *disc jockey*. Is she speaking into a microphone? (Yes)
   Look at the *reporter*. Is he talking to the cameraperson? (No)
   Find the *writer*. Is he using a typewriter? (Yes)
   Look at the *artist*. Is he rich? (Not sure)
   Look at the *architect*. Is he designing cars? (No)
   Find the *photographer*. Is he taking a picture of a model? (Yes)
   Look at the *fashion designer*. Is he designing blue jeans? (No)
   Find the *salesperson*. Is she using a cash register? (Yes)
   Look at the *newscaster*. Is she reporting good news? (Not sure)

Follow-up

5. Shuffle the occupation vocabulary index cards and pick one. Mime the occupation for the class and ask students to guess the occupation. Next, invite a volunteer to pick a card, mime the occupation on the card, and have the class guess it. Repeat the procedure three or four times, saving the remaining cards for subsequent classes.

In the Office

Focus: Identifying items used in an office.

Materials: Don't Look Mask, p. 179; listening cassette; **An Office, Dictionary, p. 83.**

Before class, duplicate and cut apart a class set of the Don't Look Mask. Look over the target vocabulary in the tapescript below.

Preview

1. Tell students that they will be listening to a person write a letter describing the people and the things he works with in his new job.
2. Direct students to open their dictionaries to page 83. Write the following three categories on the board: Job Titles, Equipment, Supplies. Elicit from students the names of occupations they see in the picture. Write the names on the board. Follow the same procedure for the other two categories. Ask students to match the occupations with the appropriate equipment and supplies as follows: secretary with telephone and calendar. Continue until all the target vocabulary in the tapescript has been mentioned.

Presentation

3. Distribute the masks and have students cover the vocabulary at the bottom of the page. Tell students to listen to the tape and to point to the correct pictures in their dictionaries. Assure students that they will have several opportunities to hear the listening passage.
4. Play the tape through "I'm a *file clerk*." Stop the tape and check to be sure that students are pointing to picture #23. Replay this section of the tape until all students are pointing to picture #23.

Practice

5. Play the tape, stopping when necessary. Replay the tape two to five times.

Follow-up

6. Check for comprehension of the target vocabulary by asking questions, such as "Where is the photocopier?" Students can respond by saying "#24" or by pointing to the correct picture.

Variation

To make the follow-up more challenging, have students, in pairs, conduct their own listen and point activity.

Tapescript (with Answers)

Listen to Alan Gordon describe his new job to his mother. Point to the items or people you hear Alan mention in his letter.

Dear Mom, How are you? I have a wonderful new job! I work for a very important company. Here's a picture of me at work. You can see I have the biggest work space (right in the middle of everything). I'm a *file clerk (23)*.* I'm in charge of all the important papers in the office. That's why I have a *photocopier (24)*. I make copies of everything important on the *photocopier (24)*.* Then I file the copies in the *file cabinet (21)*. When anyone needs those important papers, I'm the person who knows where they are.* My *manager (18)*, Ms. Lilac, has a window in her office right across from me. Sometimes when I look up, she's smiling at me. I think she likes me.* Ms. Lilac orders all the supplies and I give everyone the supplies they need. This week I told her that we need more *paper clips (28)*. (I use a lot of paper clips.)* I asked her to order another *stapler (27)*, and a *staple remover (29)*, because I only have one of each and someone is always taking them.* I always tell Ms. Lilac what we need and she uses her *calculator (19)* to figure out how many we can order.* Yesterday, she let me sit down at her *computer (16)*. I don't know anything about computers, but Mike (he's the office *typist (6)*) is going to show me how to use his *word processor (7)*. He's a great guy, Mike is, and, wow, does he type fast!* Betty, the office *secretary (11)*, is pretty nice too. She has a big *calendar (9)* on the wall over her desk and she's often on the *telephone (15)* making appointments, so she doesn't get to use her *typewriter (10)* much.* The only person in the office I don't know very well yet is Phyllis, the *switchboard operator (1)*. She's always wearing a *headset (2)*, so she's pretty hard to talk to.* Well, Mom, someone just put a *file folder (22)* on top of the *file cabinet (21)* and I have to get back to work now. This is my third week here and I'm doing fine. Who knows? Someday I may be president of this company!

Finding the Right Job

Focus: Identifying occupations by workplace and equipment.

Materials: Activity sheet, p. 137; listening cassette; notebook paper; **Occupations II, Dictionary, p. 85.**

Before class, duplicate a class set of the activity sheet. Look over the target vocabulary in the tapescript below.

Preview

1. Tell students that they will be listening to an employment counselor talk about different occupations.
2. Have students open their dictionaries to page 85 and look over the occupations. Write the occupations and these three questions on the board: Where do they work? What can they do? What do they use? Ask students to answer the questions for each occupation. Write students' answers on the board.
3. Use the information from step 2 to describe various occupations as follows: "I clean other people's houses. I use a vacuum cleaner. Who am I?" See if the class can identify which occupation you're talking about.

Presentation

4. Copy number 1 (the example) from the activity sheet onto the board. Explain the task to the students, and assure them that they will have several opportunities to hear the listening passage.
5. Play the tape through number 1, ". . . small machines. This is a job for. . . ." Stop the tape and review the example on the board.
6. Distribute the activity sheets and review the directions.

Practice

7. Play the tape, stopping after each job description. When necessary, replay each description two to five times.

8. Elicit students' responses for each occupation and get class consensus on the accuracy of the answers. Replay the tape to clarify any problems.

Follow-up

9. Divide the class into pairs and distribute the notebook paper, one sheet per pair. Have the pairs divide the paper into three columns titled: Occupations, Where do they work?, and What do they use? Have pairs brainstorm vocabulary for each column.

Tapescript (with Answers)

Listen to the employment counselor describe different occupations. Circle the correct occupation.

Good morning. We have a lot of new jobs listed this morning. I hope we can help you find one. Let me tell you about these jobs.

1. On this job you work in a factory. You put a small part on a bottle. You work next to other people who are doing the same job. Sometimes you use small machines. This is a job for. . . . *(a shop worker)*
2. Do you have any experience working in construction? On this job you build houses with wood. You use carpentry tools. This is a job for. . . . *(a carpenter)*
3. On this job you deliver food and packages to people in their homes. You bring people the things they order. You drive a delivery car. This job is for. . . . *(a delivery boy)*
4. On this job you work in a factory. You are a manager. You teach new workers what to do. You use time schedules. This is a job for. . . . *(a foreman)*
5. Do you like to work with plants and flowers? On this job, you take care of the yards outside of houses. You use gardening tools and a truck. This is a job for. . . . *(a gardener)*
6. For this job you work on the doors of houses and buildings. You put locks on the doors. Sometimes you fix locks. This is a job for. . . . *(a locksmith)*
7. Do you know anything about electricity? You put lights in buildings or repair wiring when something's wrong. You work in new buildings and houses and old ones, too. This is a job for. . . . *(an electrician)*
8. Can you fix sinks or broken toilets? You repair water pipes in houses and other buildings. You use plumbing tools. This is a job for. . . . *(a plumber)*
9. Do you know how to paint? You work on the inside and outside of buildings. You use large and small brushes. This is a job for. . . . *(a painter)*
10. On this job you work in big buildings to keep them clean. You empty the trash. You sweep the floors with a large broom. This is a job for. . . . *(a janitor)*

Main Street, USA

> **Focus:** Identifying people by their occupations.
>
> **Materials:** Activity sheet, p. 137; Don't Look Mask, p. 179; listening cassette; **Main Street USA, Dictionary, p. 84.**
>
> ---
>
> *Before class, duplicate a class set of the activity sheet and Don't Look Mask. Look over the target vocabulary in the tapescript below.*

Preview

1. Tell students that they will be listening to the owner of a florist shop talk about the people and businesses in his neighborhood.
2. Direct students to open their dictionaries to page 84. Have students look at the businesses featured on this page and identify those businesses that are within a few blocks of your school.

Presentation

3. Copy letter A (the example) from the activity sheet onto the board. Explain the task to the students, and assure them that they will have several opportunities to hear the listening passage.
4. Play the tape through letter A, "I'm a *florist*," and review the example on the board.
5. Distribute the activity sheets and masks. Have students cover the vocabulary at the bottom of the page. Review the directions.

Practice

6. Play the tape, stopping when necessary. Replay the tape two to five times.
7. Invite volunteers to do the activity at the board as you play the tape once more. Get class consensus on the accuracy of the numbers.

Follow-up

8. Check for comprehension of the target vocabulary by asking questions, such as

"Where is the *mechanic*?" Students can respond by saying "Mel's Auto Body Repair," or "#2."
9. Have student pairs ask each other about the shops in their own neighborhoods.

Variation

To make this activity more challenging, review prepositions and ask questions, such as "What shop is between the optician and the florist?"

Tapescript (with Answers)

Listen to Bob Flores talk about the people in his neighborhood. Write the number of the correct occupation.

A. Hi there! Good to see you. My name's Bob Flores. I've been on Main Street for almost six months. I'm a *florist* (11).
B. Let me tell you about some of the people on the street. Right next door to me is Magda Coleman. She's a *jeweller* from Poland. She has some beautiful rings and bracelets. (12)
C. Al is the *butcher* who's on the corner. He gave me some delicious steaks the other night. (13)
D. I love the smells when I walk by Milo's bakery. He's the *baker* on the other corner. Sometimes I stop by and pick up a loaf of bread on my way home. (8)
E. Last week my car broke down and I took it over to Mel's Auto Body Repair. Mel's an excellent *mechanic*. He sure fixed my car fast and he's not expensive either. (2)
F. When I need a haircut, I go round the corner to see Pete Garabedian. He runs the *barber* shop. Everybody stops in to say hello at Pete's place. (3)
G. I usually buy my fruits and vegetables from Kim Nguyen, the *greengrocer* down the street from Pete. She has the best apples anywhere. (7)
H. If you ever need to fix a TV, go see Maggie. She's a terrific *repairperson*. She can fix anything. My old stereo never sounded so good! (5)
I. Today, I met another new business owner, Robert Chen. He makes eyeglasses. He's the *optician* who just moved in two stores west of me. (9)
J. My clothes are always too big, so I take them to the *tailor* shop around the corner. Susie Lew runs it and she sews beautifully. (6)
K. When things are slow, sometimes I go and talk to Julie. She's the *hairdresser* who works right next door. You should see some of the beautiful hairstyles she does on her customers. (10)
L. Let's see. Who else is in my neighborhood? Oh, yes. I almost forgot about Nancy. She's the *pharmacist* on the corner next to Mel's. When I hurt my back, Nancy told me what medicine would help—and it did. (1)
M. When I want to travel, I can go over to Global Tours to see Gloria. She's a *travel agent*. She knows a lot of wonderful places to visit. Well, guess I'd better get back to work. Please stop by soon. (4)

Job Openings

Focus: Asking for and giving information about job openings.

Materials: Activity sheet, p. 138; manila folders (one per pair); **Farming and Ranching, Construction, An Office,** and **Occupations I, II,** and **III, Dictionary, pp. 81–86.**

Before class, duplicate half a class set of the activity sheet. Cut apart the A and B sections of the sheets and keep them separate. Copy the questions and headings (Job, Hourly Wage, Hours) from the activity sheet onto the board.

Preview

1. Tell students that they will be working in pairs to find out the missing information about job openings.
2. Have students brainstorm the names of several jobs they know. Write the job names on the board under the "Job" heading. Ask students for hourly wages and hours for these jobs and write this information on the board under the appropriate headings.

Presentation

3. Use the questions on the board to model the language and clarification strategy you want students to use in the activity. Have the class practice asking and answering the questions for different jobs.
4. Pair students and assign each one an A or a B role. Explain to students that they will each have a job board with some wages and hours missing. Point out that the missing information is on their partner's job board. Tell students that they will take turns asking for and giving the missing information in order to complete their boards.
5. Distribute a manila folder to each pair, to be propped up between the students as a screen. Distribute the A and B activity sheets to the appropriate partners. Review the directions and instruct students to look only

at their own papers and not at their partner's.
6. Tell students to look at the example on their job boards and to tell you the hourly wage for the security guard. Check comprehension by asking A students, "What's the hourly wage for the teller?" Ask B students, "What are the hours for the teller?"
7. Have one pair demonstrate the activity by asking for and giving one additional piece of missing information from their job boards. Remind students to look only at their own papers.

Practice

8. Have students, in pairs, ask and answer questions about the missing information on their activity sheets. Once they complete the task, partners can compare job boards to be sure they are the same.

Follow-up

9. Have pairs form groups of four to create four additional job openings. Tell students to use the pages in their dictionaries and their completed job boards as reference.

Office Supplies

Focus: Giving and following directions for placing items in an office.

Materials: Office items, such as envelopes, pencils, staplers, staple removers, paper clips, file folders, calendars, calculators, large manila envelopes; 8-1/2" × 14" pads of paper; message pads; 8-1/2" × 11" sheets of lined paper; **An Office, and Prepositions of Description, Dictionary, pp. 83 and 102.**

Before class, gather the office items. You'll need three items for each group.

Preview

1. Tell students that they will be giving and following directions for placing office items on a desk.
2. Direct students to open their dictionaries to page 102 to review prepositions of description. Then have students turn to page 83 and discuss the location of the items on the table in back of the file clerk (#23), using the prepositions. Ask questions, such as "Where's the photocopier?" and "Where's the pencil sharpener?"
3. Have students tell you how to place items on a table like the one pictured in the dictionary. As students direct you ("Put the legal pad next to the paper clips."), carry out their directions using your desk or a classroom table and the actual items. Incorporate appropriate clarification questions as you respond to the directions, such as "Where?"; "Next to what?"; or "In front of what?"
4. Invite volunteers to place several items according to your directions.

Presentation

5. Ask two of your more advanced students to come to the front of the room. Call one student the "manager" and the other the "file clerk." Have the manager give the file clerk directions to place several of the items. Encourage the class to help both students complete their tasks.

Practice

6. Group four to six students together and distribute one sheet of blank paper to each group. Have one representative from each group choose three office items and take them back to his group. Instruct the groups to think of four to six directions (TPR commands) for placing their three items, such as "Put the envelope on top of the file folder," or "Put the stapler between the pencil and the paper clips." Have each group appoint one student to write the commands on the sheet of paper.
7. Ask each group to choose an office manager. Have the office managers take their group's items and list of commands and move to another group. Tell the managers to give their new groups the commands for individual students to carry out. When every student in that group has had a turn, rotate the managers once again. Continue rotating until all the managers return to their original groups.

Follow-up

8. Compile a class list of all the commands and write them on slips of paper. Divide the class into two teams and put all the office supplies on a table in the front. Invite two volunteers from one team to the front. Have one student pick a cue slip and tell his teammate how to arrange the supplies on the table. Have the other team verify the first team's accuracy. If the items are placed correctly, the first team gets a point. If they are placed incorrectly, the other team has a chance to get the point. Teams continue taking turns picking cue slips until one team has ten points.

Occupation Go Around

Preview

1. Tell students that they are going to test their knowledge of occupations by playing a board game with their classmates.
2. Direct students to open their dictionaries to pages 84 and 85. Write the following statements and questions on the board: "Say it and spell it," "Where do you do this job?"; "What can this worker do?"; and "What tools do you use for this job?" Ask the class to choose one occupation from pages 84 and 85 and to respond to each statement or question on the board.

Presentation

3. Copy the activity sheet onto the board, filling in only the first four squares. Put the 8-1/2" x 11" occupation pictures on the chalk ledge, face down. Invite three volunteers to the front of the room. Have the volunteers write their names on separate pieces of scratch paper, while you do the same. Tape the papers to the "Start" square. Explain that the papers are the game markers.
4. Show the class a coin and demonstrate flipping it "heads" and "tails." Flip the coin and move your marker on the board, one

space for heads, two spaces for tails. Move your marker to the square "Pick a card: Say it and spell it," or "Name your occupation." Have the class read the directions aloud. Follow the directions. Play two rounds of the game with the three volunteers. Get class consensus on the accuracy of the volunteers' responses. Point out that when a response is not correct, the player cannot flip the coin on his next turn and must answer the same question again.

Practice

5. Divide the class into groups of four. Distribute the activity sheets (game boards), picture card sets, coins, and scratch paper to each group. Have each group create four "markers" and place them on the "Start" square.
6. Check for general understanding of the game by asking yes/no questions, such as "Do I move two spaces for heads?" and "Do I pick a card from the top of the pile?"
7. Set a 20-minute time limit for the game and begin play.
8. Circulate and monitor student practice. (In cases where groups cannot come to consensus, you serve as referee.)

Follow-up

9. Divide the class into two teams, A and B. Copy the activity sheet onto the board, replacing the directions with numbers. Have team members take turns flipping coins and answering your questions (the original questions or new ones).

Variation

Divide the class into groups of five. Students 1 and 2 form team A, students 3 and 4 form team B, and student 5 serves as the referee. Proceed as before (step 9). Allow referees to use the dictionary and other resources to decide if spelling and other responses are accurate.

Apply Yourself

> **Focus:** Asking for and giving personal information in a job interview.
>
> **Materials:** Activity sheet, p. 140; **Occupations III, Dictionary, p. 86.**
>
> *Before class, duplicate a class set of the activity sheet.*

Preview

1. Tell students that they will be applying for jobs or interviewing applicants at an employment agency, of which you are the manager.
2. Ask students about the kinds of questions job applicants need to answer in an interview, such as "What's your name?"; "What was your last job?"; and "Can you operate a photocopier?" Write suggested questions on the board.
3. Practice asking and answering job interview questions with the class. Use the questions generated in step 2 as a guide.

Presentation

4. Divide the class in half. Assign one half the role of "applicants" and the other half the role of employment agency "counselors." Have the applicants form pairs and the counselors form groups of four.
5. Distribute the activity sheets. Instruct the applicants to help each other complete the activity sheet by writing in or circling the appropriate information. Have the counselors work together to create appropriate questions for the form (Name: What's your name?). Give students 15 minutes to complete this activity. Collect the forms from the applicants only.
6. Set up a table in front of the room and list the following steps on the board:
   a. Introduce yourself
   b. Shake hands
   c. Invite applicant to sit down
   d. Ask and answer questions
   e. Say goodbye
   f. Thank the counselor.

Invite one counselor and one applicant to role play an interview using the steps on the board. Encourage the class to assist the actors over any rough spots. Review any special language problems that arose during the demonstration (step 5) <u>before proceeding with the role play</u>.

Practice

7. Arrange the classroom so that counselors and applicants are seated face to face. Direct two counselors and two applicants to form a group of four. Have one counselor/applicant pair proceed with the steps of the role play, while the other pair observes and assists. After the first pair completes its turn, have the students observe and assist the second pair's role play.
8. Circulate as employment manager, monitoring the interviews. Encourage groups who finish quickly to switch roles. End the role play when all the pairs have completed their interviews.

Follow-up

9. Invite a volunteer from each group to list her own or her partner's skills on the board. Direct students to open their dictionaries to pages 81–87. Have students use the information on the board and the occupations in the dictionary to decide upon the best job for each of the applicants identified on the board.

Your Notes

Finding the Right Job (See Teacher's Notes, page 130.)

- Listen to the employment counselor describe different occupations.
- Circle the correct occupation.

1.	a janitor	(a shop worker)	a carpenter
2.	a shop worker	a plumber	a carpenter
3.	an electrician	a delivery boy	a foreman
4.	a gardener	a foreman	a locksmith
5.	a plumber	a gardener	a shop worker
6.	a delivery boy	a painter	a locksmith
7.	an electrician	a janitor	a painter
8.	a plumber	an electrician	a carpenter
9.	a foreman	a gardener	a painter
10.	a locksmith	a delivery boy	a janitor

- ✂

Main Street, USA (See Teacher's Notes, page 131.)

- Listen to Bob Flores talk about the people in his neighborhood.
- Write the number of the correct occupation.

A. __11__   F. _____   K. _____

B. _____   G. _____   L. _____

C. _____   H. _____   M. _____

D. _____   I. _____

E. _____   J. _____

Job Openings (See Teacher's Notes, page 132.)

- Look at the job board below.
- Take turns asking your partner these kinds of questions:
    - What's the hourly wage for the _____ (job)?
    - What are the hours for the _____ (job)?
- Write in the missing information.
- When you don't hear an answer, say "Tell me again, please."

A

—= JOB =—	—= HOURLY WAGE =—	—= HOURS =—
Security guard	$7.50 an hour	11:00 PM - 7:00 AM
Teller	$8.00 an hour	
Receptionist		8:30 AM - 5:30 PM
Salesperson	$5.50 an hour	
Computer programmer		7:00 AM - 3:00 PM
Accountant	$12.00 an hour	

- Look at the job board below.
- Take turns asking your partner these kinds of questions:
    - What's the hourly wage for the _____ (job)?
    - What are the hours for the _____ (job)?
- Write in the missing information.
- When you don't hear an answer, say "Tell me again, please."

B

—= JOB =—	—= HOURLY WAGE =—	—= HOURS =—
Security guard	$7.50 an hour	11:00 PM - 7:00 AM
Teller		8:00 AM - 4:00 PM
Receptionist	$9.00 an hour	
Salesperson		3:00 PM - 9:00 PM
Computer programmer	$18.00 an hour	
Accountant		9:00 AM - 5:00 PM

Occupation Go Around (See Teacher's Notes, page 134.)

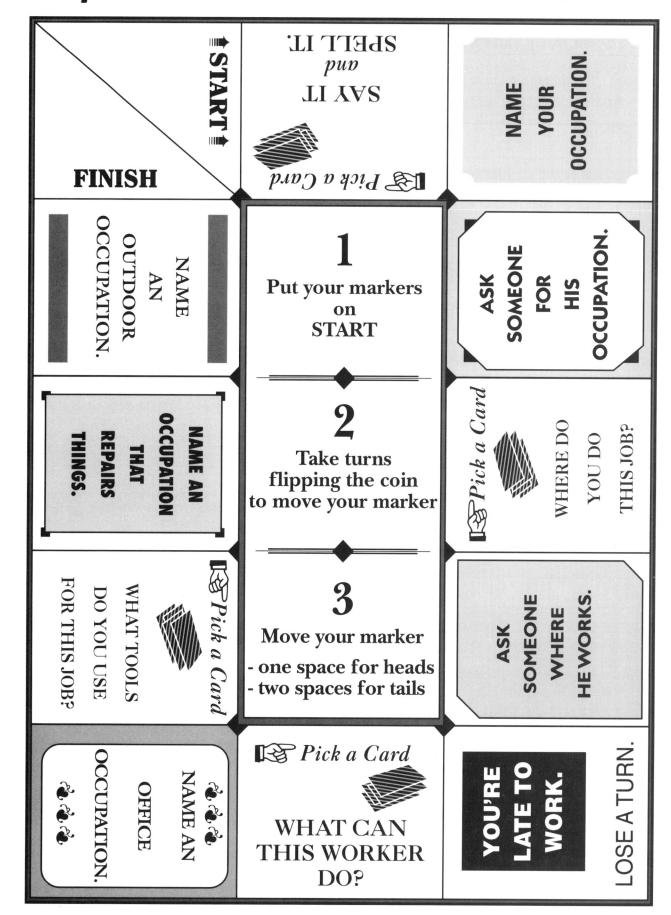

START →

Pick a Card ☞

SAY IT
and
SPELL IT.

NAME YOUR OCCUPATION.

FINISH

NAME AN OUTDOOR OCCUPATION.

ASK SOMEONE FOR HIS OCCUPATION.

1
Put your markers on START

2
Take turns flipping the coin to move your marker

3
Move your marker
- one space for heads
- two spaces for tails

NAME AN OCCUPATION THAT REPAIRS THINGS.

☞ *Pick a Card*
WHERE DO YOU DO THIS JOB?

☞ *Pick a Card*
WHAT TOOLS DO YOU USE FOR THIS JOB?

ASK SOMEONE WHERE HE WORKS.

NAME AN OFFICE OCCUPATION.

☞ *Pick a Card*
WHAT CAN THIS WORKER DO?

YOU'RE LATE TO WORK.

LOSE A TURN.

Apply Yourself (See Teacher's Notes, page 135.)

PERSONAL INFORMATION

Name: _____

Address: _____

Phone: _____

EXPERIENCE

Occupation: _____

Last job: _____

SKILLS:

bake	yes	no
cook	yes	no
cut hair	yes	no
drive a car	yes	no
drive a truck	yes	no
drive a bus	yes	no
file	yes	no
operate a camera	yes	no
operate a computer	yes	no
ride a horse	yes	no
sew	yes	no
type	yes	no
use a calculator	yes	no
use a cash register	yes	no
use gardening equipment	yes	no
use a jackhammer	yes	no
other	_____	

LANGUAGES

_____

English   Spanish   Chinese   Japanese   French   Farsi   Arabic   Other

Enjoying Free Time
Teacher's Notes and Activity Sheets

Activity Title	■ Activity Type	Page
A Day at the Beach Students look at a beach scene in the Dictionary and respond to a series of yes/no questions.	■ Silent Drill	142
Taking Care of Alex Students listen to a mother giving instructions to a babysitter and point to the correct pictures in the Dictionary.	■ Listen and Point	143
Sports Highlights Students listen to a sports announcer talking about different sports and circle the correct sports.	■ Listen and Circle	144
The Great Outdoors Students listen to people talking about different activities at a campsite and check the correct activity.	■ Listening Grid	145
What's the Next Event? Students complete identical sports event schedules by asking for and giving times, events, and countries.	■ Information Gap	146
Sports Survey Students exchange and record information about sports preferences and compile a class survey.	■ Interview	147
We Can Do It All Students circulate to find classmates who can do various actions.	■ Class Search	148
Friendship Quilt Students design and sew a quilt and write a description of the experience.	■ Language Experience	149

Reproducible activity sheets on pages 151–154.

A Day at the Beach

Focus: Identifying items at the beach.

Materials: Answer Cards and Don't Look Mask, p. 179; **At the Beach, Dictionary, pp. 90–91.**

Before class, duplicate and cut apart a class set of the Answer Cards and Don't Look Mask. Look over the silent drill questions and the target vocabulary (step 4 below).

Preview

1. Hold up a set of answer cards and tell students that they will be listening to and answering a series of questions by raising the correct answer card.
2. Direct students to open their dictionaries to pages 90 and 91. Ask students to identify the people and the items on the pages (lifeguard, swimmer, beach ball, kite). Talk about what the people are doing and what the items are used for.

Presentation

3. Distribute the answer cards and masks. Have students cover the vocabulary at the bottom of the two pages and listen to your questions about the pictures. Ask the first question: "Is the *lifeguard* looking through *binoculars?*" Tell students to raise the Yes card if the answer is yes, the No card if it is no, and the Not Sure card when there's not enough information to answer yes or no. Get class consensus on the first answer before continuing.

Practice (with Answers)

4. Ask the following questions:
   Is the *lifeguard* looking through *binoculars?* (No)
   Is the man under the *beach umbrella* wearing *sunglasses?* (Yes)
   Are two men playing with the *Frisbee?* (No)
   Is anyone wearing the *scuba tank* and the *wet suit?* (No)
   Are there five people in the *water?* (Yes)
   Is the *lifeboat* next to the *lifeguard?* (Yes)
   Is the woman in the red *bathing suit* using *suntan lotion?* (Yes)
   Are two brothers building a *sandcastle?* (Not sure)
   Is there a man selling hot dogs at the *refreshment stand?* (Yes)
   Are there five *beach chairs* at this beach? (No)

Follow-up

5. Have students talk about the conversations that might be taking place. Ask students to identify the people and what each person is saying.

Taking Care of Alex

Focus: Identifying locations in a park.

Materials: Don't Look Mask, p. 179; listening cassette; **Neighborhood Parks, Dictionary, p. 87.**

Before class, duplicate a set of the Don't Look Mask. Look over the target vocabulary in the tapescript below.

Preview

1. Tell students that they will be listening to a woman talking to her son's babysitter.
2. Direct students to open their dictionaries to page 87. Ask students to identify 10 locations in the park that children would like. List their choices on the board and add any target vocabulary that is missing.

Presentation

3. Distribute the masks and have students cover the vocabulary at the bottom of the page. Tell students to listen to the tape and to point to the correct pictures in their dictionaries. Assure students that they will have several opportunities to hear the listening passage.
4. Play the tape through "So, go to the *zoo* first." Stop the tape and check to be sure that students are pointing to picture #1. Replay this section of the tape until all students are pointing to picture #1.

Practice

5. Play the tape, stopping when necessary. Replay the tape two to five times.

Follow-up

6. Check for comprehension of the target vocabulary by asking questions, such as "Where is the man in the hat?" Students can respond by giving the location or by pointing to the correct picture.

Variation

To make the follow-up more challenging, have student pairs create a dialogue between the babysitter and the boy, Alex. Replay the tape if students want to clarify vocabulary.

Tapescript (with Answers)

Listen while Sara tells her son's baby-sitter what to do at the park with Alex. Point to the places you hear Sara talking about.

Hi, Joan. Alex is really excited about going to the park. He loves to feed the animals. So, go to the *zoo (1)* first. Here are some peanuts for the elephants.* The *duck pond (8)* is right in front of the zoo. Alex loves the ducks. Here are some crackers for them.* Then buy Alex some ice cream. The *ice cream vendor (3)* is always by the pond. Here's some money for that.* If you go to the *jungle gym (17)*, stay near Alex. He can climb to the top by himself, but he can't always climb down.* If he goes on the *seesaw (18)*, stand close to him. He gets scared when it goes up.* If he wants to go on the *slide (12)*, fine, but please wait at the bottom for him.* Alex loves the *swings (16)*. He can go on the swings by himself, but help him get on and get off.* Near the swings is the *sprinkler (14)*. Don't let him get wet! He hates it when his clothes are wet.* Sometimes he sees a *horseback rider (6)* on the *bridle path (7)*. He loves horses.* If he sees a horse and gets excited, take him to the *merry-go-round (5)*. He likes the purple horse the best.* Let's see, did I forget anything? Oh, yes, the *sandbox (13)*. Take him to the sandbox last, at the end of the afternoon.* You know why? There's a nice *bench (10)* next to it. It's the only bench in the park, and by that time, you'll need it!

Sports Highlights

> **Focus:** Identifying individual sports.
>
> **Materials:** Activity sheet, p. 151; listening cassette; **Individual Sports, Dictionary, p. 94.**
>
> ---
>
> *Before class, duplicate a class set of the activity sheet. Look over the target vocabulary in the tapescript below.*

Preview

1. Tell students that they will be listening to a sports announcer give the weekend sports news.
2. Direct students to open their dictionaries to page 94. Name different kinds of sports equipment and find out from students the sport for which each is used. Have students look at the page and identify sports that are popular in their countries.

Presentation

3. Copy number 1 (the example) from the activity sheet onto the board. Explain the task to students, and assure them that they will have several opportunities to hear the listening passage.
4. Play the tape through number 1, ". . . and is ready to serve the *tennis ball*." Stop the tape and review the example on the board.
5. Distribute the activity sheets and review the directions.

Practice

6. Play the tape, stopping after each item. When necessary, replay each item two to five times.
7. Elicit students' responses for each item and get class consensus on the accuracy of the answers. Replay the tape to clarify any problems.

Follow-up

8. Have students work in groups of four to brainstorm the names of the closest place to school where they might be able to play some of the sports. Share the information with the class.

Tapescript (with Answers)

Listen to the sports announcer talk about different sports. Circle the correct sport.

1. The crowd is quiet for the third match. Wilma has her *tennis racket* above her head and is ready to serve the *tennis ball*. *(tennis)*
2. Tanya Green is an outstanding *gymnast*, ladies and gentlemen. See her standing on the *balance beam* now. She's getting ready to jump off. Let's watch. *(gymnastics)*
3. This is a close match. Here is Jerry Lee getting ready to return the *Ping-Pong ball*. He is holding the *paddle* tightly in his right hand. *(Ping-Pong)*
4. Experienced golfer Neil Atwater is very upset! His *golf ball* just missed the *hole!* Maybe he needs to change his *putter*. *(golf)*
5. This is the first tournament for Eric and Steve Sutton. They always wear *safety goggles* and use their best *racquets* when they play doubles. Good luck, guys! *(racquetball)*
6. Tim Jackins is going for the championship tonight. The *rink* is in good condition, but he looks a little wobbly on those *skates*. Let's watch him go for the final spin. *(ice skating)*
7. Donna Diaz is looking very good tonight. The *bowling ball* is going straight down the *lane* for a spare. Way to go, Donna! *(bowling)*
8. Ralph Jurgens has strong legs and will surely win this *cross-country skiing* race. He uses long *skis* and two short *poles*. He is an excellent skier. *(cross-country skiing)*
9. The race is very close. Billy Boots is a good *jockey*, but he's riding too far back in the *saddle*. He's got to loosen up on the reins if he's going to win this one. *(horse racing)*
10. There's Florence Jackson finishing the mile relay. This is her second win on the same *track* in less than a week. She's a fast *runner* and she's got a big smile on her face. Congratulations, Florence. *(track and field)*

The Great Outdoors

Focus: Identifying different outdoor activities.

Materials: Activity sheet, p. 151; listening cassette; **Outdoor Activities, Dictionary, pp. 88–89.**

Before class, duplicate a class set of the activity sheet. Look over the target vocabulary in the tapescript below.

Preview

1. Tell students that they will be listening to people doing different outdoor activities.
2. Direct students to open their dictionaries to pages 88 and 89. Ask students to identify the different activities on the page: fishing, rafting, mountain climbing, and camping, and talk about what vocabulary goes with each activity.

Presentation

3. Copy number 1 (the example) from the activity sheet onto the board. Explain the task to students, and assure them that they will have several opportunities to hear the listening passage.
4. Play the tape through number 1, ". . . when we get there." Stop the tape and review the example on the board.
5. Distribute the activity sheets and review the directions.

Practice

6. Play the tape, stopping after each item. When necessary, replay each item two to five times.
7. Elicit students' responses for each item, and get class consensus on the accuracy of the answers. Replay the tape to clarify problems.

Follow-up

8. Have students, in pairs, role play one of the activities on the page: catching a fish, rafting, climbing a mountain, camping. Ask student volunteers to share their conversations.

Tapescript (with Answers)

Listen to the people talking about different outdoor activities. Check the correct activity.

1. Here, Ralph. Grab the *rope*. We're almost to the top of the *peak*. I'll bet we can see a lot when we get there. *(mountain climbing)*
2. I'm glad the *waterfall* is behind us, John. Let's paddle to the right. There aren't any *rapids* that way. *(rafting)*
3. I've got one! I've got one! What a beauty! I hope my *fishing net* doesn't have a hole in it. *(fishing)*
4. Here, I brought some wood for the *campfire*. Anybody have any marshmallows to roast? *(camping)*
5. Put the lantern near my *sleeping bag*, Al. I brought a book that I want to read. *(camping)*
6. Can't you make this *raft* go any slower? I feel sick and the water is rough. *(rafting)*
7. I need to stop. I want to check my *harness* and my *rope*. This *mountain* is harder than I thought. *(mountain climbing)*
8. Darn! That fish ate my bait. Look—there's nothing on my *fishing line*. I'm glad it didn't eat my *fishing rod* too. *(fishing)*
9. I think it's going to rain. We'd better put the *gear* in the *tent* now. And the *lantern*—we'd better put that inside too. *(camping)*
10. So, what do you think? It's a beautiful night tonight. I say we take the *sleeping bags* out of the *tents* and sleep on the ground. *(camping)*

What's the Next Event?

> **Focus:** Asking for and giving schedule information.
>
> **Materials:** Activity sheet, p. 152; manila folders (one per pair); **Team Sports,** and **Individual Sports, Dictionary, pp. 92 and 94.**
>
> _Before class, duplicate half a class set of the activity sheet. Cut apart the A and B sections of the sheets and keep them separate. Copy the questions from the activity sheet onto the board._

Preview

1. Tell students that they will be working in pairs to find out information on a schedule for one day at the Olympics.
2. Direct students to open their dictionaries to pages 92 and 94. Have students brainstorm the names of sports played at the Summer Olympics. Ask students to identify the countries that do well in these sports. Add countries from the activity sheet.

Presentation

3. Use the questions on the board to model the language and clarification strategy you want students to use in the activity. Have students practice the questions, substituting different times, sports, and countries.
4. Pair students and assign each one an A or B role. Explain to students that they will each have a schedule with various times, sports, and names of countries missing. Tell students that they will take turns asking for and giving the missing information in order to complete their schedules.
5. Distribute a manila folder to each pair, to be propped up between the students as a screen. Distribute the A and B activity sheets to the appropriate partners. Instruct students to look only at their own papers and not at their partner's.

6. Tell students to look at the example on their schedules and to tell you what sport is at 11:00. Check comprehension by asking A students, "What countries are playing baseball?" Ask B students, "What countries are playing basketball?"
7. Have one pair demonstrate the activity by asking for and giving one additional piece of missing information from their schedules. Remind students to look only at their own papers.

Practice

8. Have students, in pairs, ask and answer questions about the missing information on their schedules. Once they complete the task, partners can compare schedules to be sure they are the same.

Follow-up

9. Have students discuss which sports they would prefer to watch. Have them talk about which sports they would prefer to play.

Sports Survey

Focus: Discussing sports preferences.

Materials: Activity sheet, p. 153; **Team Sports,** and **Individual Sports, Dictionary, pp. 92 and 94.**

Before class, duplicate a class set of the activity sheet.

Preview

1. Tell students that they will be interviewing their classmates and talking about sports preferences.
2. Direct students to open their dictionaries to pages 92 and 94. Ask students what sports they have played. Write students' answers on the board.

Presentation

3. Copy the grid from the activity sheet onto the board. Model the questions for each space on the grid: "What's your favorite sport to watch?"; "What's your favorite sport to play?"; and so on. Using the grid on the board, write your name in the first column and have the class ask you the first question. Answer the question about yourself and write your answer in the grid box. Explain that only short answers are written in the boxes below the questions.
4. Ask a volunteer to come to the board. Write the student's name under your name on the grid. Have different students ask the volunteer one question each from the grid. Write the answers on the grid.

Practice

5. Divide the class into groups of five and distribute an activity sheet to each student.
6. Have students take turns asking the questions of the person on their left, while the other group members listen and write the answers on their grids. When students have completed their grids, they can use the information to discuss the questions below the grid.

7. Set a 20-minute time limit for students to complete the task. Circulate and monitor student practice.

Follow-up

8. Use the grid on the board to elicit responses from each group. Number the groups and write the group numbers in the first column. Ask the survey questions and write the groups' responses on the board. Continue asking the groups all the questions, writing the single majority response wherever possible. If each group member has a different answer, write "varies."
9. When you've finished interviewing all the groups, have students use your completed survey to comment on patterns in the class.

Variations

To make the activity easier, conduct a teacher-directed survey with the whole class.

To make the activity more challenging, have groups generate three additional items to include in their surveys.

We Can Do It All

> ***Focus:*** Asking and responding to information questions.
>
> ***Materials:*** Activity sheet, p. 153; **Sports Verbs, Dictionary, pp. 96–97.**
>
> *Before class, duplicate a class set of the activity sheet.*

Preview

1. Tell students that they will be searching for classmates who can perform certain sports activities.
2. Direct students to open their dictionaries to pages 96 and 97. Survey the class, asking questions, such as "How many of you can hit a baseball?" or "How many can ride a horse?" (You can also repeat the verb and just vary the noun, such as "How many can ride a motorcycle?"; "How many can ride a bicycle?")

Presentation

3. Model the following questions: "Can you kick a soccer ball?"; "Can you bounce a basketball?"; and so on. Pantomime the answers: "Yes, I can" (show the action) or "No, I can't."
4. Copy the first two action phrases from the activity sheet onto the board. Ask the class the first question until a volunteer answers, "Yes, I can" as her answer. Say, "Show me," and have the student pantomime the correct action (with your help, if necessary). Then have the student write her name on the line next to the first action phrase on the board.
5. Have another student ask the class the second question, and proceed until a second student correctly pantomimes the action and writes her name on the line next to the second phrase on the board.

Practice

6. Distribute an activity sheet to each student. Have students walk around the room getting as many different student signatures as possible.
7. As students complete their entire activity sheet, they may sit down.

Follow-up

8. To find out who can do the different actions, survey the class asking questions, such as "Who found someone who can surf?" Discuss which actions are the most difficult and which are the easiest.

Variation

To make this activity more challenging, have students who answer, "Yes, I can," elaborate by stating a condition, such as "I catch a baseball when I play first base."

Friendship Quilt

Focus: Making and describing a class quilt.

Materials: Activity sheet, p. 154; light-colored, plain woven 35"–45" fabric—preferably cotton (one yard for every nine students); one pair of scissors; two needles; pins; thread (one spool per group); fabric crayons or permanent colored markers; chalk; 8-1/2" x 11" sheets of blank paper; one large sheet of butcher paper (approximately 2' x 3'); **Handicrafts, Dictionary, p. 101.**

Before class on the first day, duplicate a class set of the activity sheet. Cut apart the grid and the directions and keep them separate. Collect extra fabric and supplies for those students who may not be able to bring them.

Preview (Day 1)

1. Tell students that they will be constructing a friendship quilt and will later write about how it was done.
2. Direct students to open their dictionaries to page 101. Review the names of sewing items and talk about the woman pictured quilting (#32).
3. Divide students into groups of four and distribute the activity sheet. Have each member of the group take turns asking, "Can you bring . . . ?"-questions for the materials needed for class the next day.
4. Decide as a class what kind of theme your class quilt will have. Some possibilities are: flags of different countries, friendship sayings, student drawings with symbols representing the students' lives. Or the quilt can be free-form.

Presentation (Day 2)

5. Have students re-form their groups from Day 1. Distribute the 8-1/2" x 11" sheets of blank paper and have students draw out the design for their squares. Have students share in their groups what they drew and tell why it is interesting to them.
6. Distribute the bottom portion (directions) of the activity sheet. Have each group choose a "head tailor" to be the group's leader.
7. Call the head tailors to the front of the room and demonstrate the various steps of the directions. Explain the vocabulary including, edges, right side of the fabric, wrong side of the fabric, sew, and pin.
8. Have students read over the directions while the head tailors demonstrate the actions to their groups. Be sure each group has enough supplies and fabric.

Practice

9. Circulate to help all students participate in the activity. Encourage students to come to you if they need assistance.

Follow-up

10. Post the large butcher paper at the front of the room. Ask students what steps they followed to make the friendship quilt. Write the steps on the board exactly as the students tell them to you. Have students read the steps and copy them.

   The following is a typical level-one story: We sew a friendship quilt. We put a picture on the paper and copy the picture. We use crayons to make the picture. We sew the quilt and put together it. We put the quilt on the wall. It is very beautiful.

Your Notes

Sports Highlights (See Teacher's Notes, page 144.)

■ Listen to the sports announcer talk about different sports.
■ Circle the correct sport.

1.	boxing	(tennis)	horse racing
2.	gymnastics	Ping-Pong	racquetball
3.	handball	ice skating	Ping-Pong
4.	golf	bowling	boxing
5.	horse racing	skiing	racquetball
6.	track and field	ice skating	bowling
7.	bowling	boxing	handball
8.	golf	cross-country skiing	gymnastics
9.	tennis	boxing	horse racing
10.	track and field	gymnastics	handball

- ✂

The Great Outdoors (See Teacher's Notes, page 145.)

■ Listen to the people talking about different outdoor activities.
■ Check (√) the correct activity.

1			√	
2				
3				
4				
5				
6				
7				
8				
9				
10				

What's the Next Event? (See Teacher's Notes, page 146.)

- Look at the schedule.
- Take turns asking your partner these kinds of questions:
  - What time is _____ (event)?
  - What event is at _____ (time)?
  - What countries are playing _____ (sport)?

- Write in the missing information.
- When you don't understand an answer, ask "What did you say?"

A

TODAY'S SCHEDULE

TIME	EVENT	COUNTRIES
11:00	Boxing	Korea and United States
	Baseball	Japan and Venezuela
1:45		
	Volleyball	
4:30		Mexico and Brazil

✂

- Look at the schedule.
- Take turns asking your partner these kinds of questions:
  - What time is _____ (event)?
  - What event is at _____ (time)?
  - What countries are playing _____ (sport)?

- Write in the missing information.
- When you don't understand an answer, ask "What did you say?"

B

TODAY'S SCHEDULE

TIME	EVENT	COUNTRIES
11:00	Boxing	
12:30		
	Basketball	Norway and Poland
3:15		France
	Soccer	Mexico and Brazil

Sports Survey (See Teacher's Notes, page 147.)

- Work in small groups.
- Take turns asking and answering the questions on the grid below.
- Record the answers on the grid.

NAME	What's your favorite sport to watch?	What's your favorite sport to play?	What's the most difficult sport to play?	Where do you go to watch sports?

- After you complete the grid, discuss these questions with your group:
   Is there a difference between men's and women's answers?
   Is there a sport that is popular to watch in your group?
   Is there a sport that is popular to play in your group?

-- ✂

We Can Do It All (See Teacher's Notes, page 148.)

- Go around the room finding classmates who can do each action.
- Say "Show me," when you find someone who can do it.
- Have the person sign his/her name in the correct space.

1. _____ can catch a baseball.

2. _____ can throw a tennis ball.

3. _____ can ride a horse.

4. _____ can shoot an arrow.

5. _____ can jump in the air.

6. _____ can fall down.

7. _____ can run around a chair.

8. _____ can bounce a basketball.

9. _____ can dive into a pool.

10. _____ can skate with ice skates.

11. _____ can catch a football.

12. _____ can drive a truck.

Friendship Quilt (See Teacher's Notes, page 149.)

■ Ask "Can you bring . . . ?" questions.
■ Check (√) the supplies each person can bring.

NAME	FABRIC	SCISSORS	PINS	THREAD	NEEDLES	MARKERS/CRAYONS

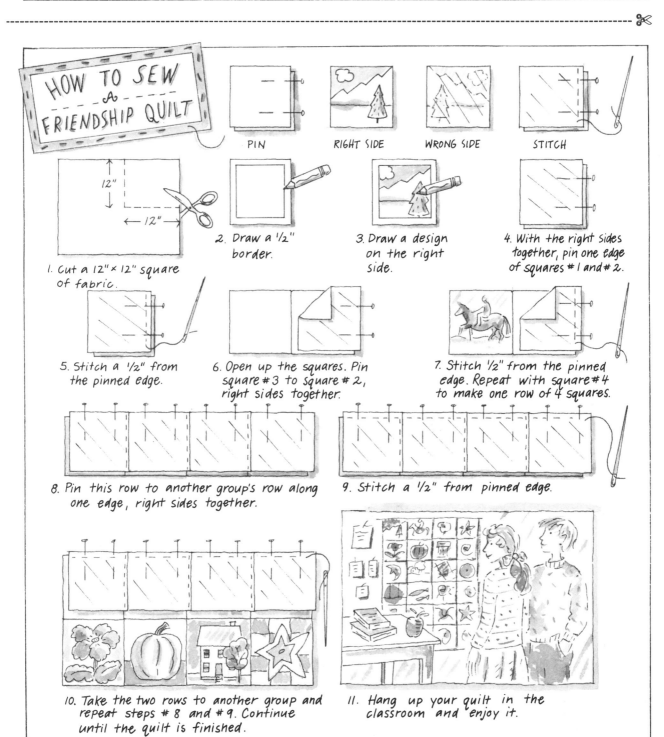

HOW TO SEW A FRIENDSHIP QUILT

PIN   RIGHT SIDE   WRONG SIDE   STITCH

1. Cut a 12" × 12" square of fabric.

2. Draw a ½" border.

3. Draw a design on the right side.

4. With the right sides together, pin one edge of squares #1 and #2.

5. Stitch a ½" from the pinned edge.

6. Open up the squares. Pin square #3 to square #2, right sides together.

7. Stitch ½" from the pinned edge. Repeat with square #4 to make one row of 4 squares.

8. Pin this row to another group's row along one edge, right sides together.

9. Stitch a ½" from pinned edge.

10. Take the two rows to another group and repeat steps #8 and #9. Continue until the quilt is finished.

11. Hang up your quilt in the classroom and enjoy it.

All-Around Activities
Teacher's Notes and Activity Sheets

Reproducible activity sheets on pages 173–176.

Grandma Jones

> **Focus:** Using vocabulary in a substitution drill.
>
> **Materials:** Dictionary pages for reference.
>
> ───────────────────────────
>
> *Before class, choose the Dictionary topic and vocabulary you want to review.*

Preview

1. Tell students that they will be talking about Grandma Jones, who has everything, can do everything, and goes everywhere. Announce the dictionary topic of the day and write a corresponding statement on the board, such as "In Grandma's fruit bowl there are some apples," or "Grandma's going to the bank."
2. Direct students to the appropriate dictionary pages and have them practice making sentences using the model statement on the board.

Presentation

3. Have students close their dictionaries. Model a sentence from step 2 ("In Grandma's fruit bowl there are some apples."), and have students repeat it. Add another vocabulary item to your first sentence. ("In Grandma's fruit bowl there are some apples and some bananas."), and have students repeat the new sentence.
4. Ask a student, "What's in your Grandma Jones' kitchen?" Help the student repeat the previous sentence, adding a new vocabulary item at the end. Then have the class repeat the chain, which now has three items.
5. Have Student 1 ask another student, "What's in Grandma Jones' kitchen?" This next student repeats the three previous items and adds her own. The whole class repeats the entire chain.

Practice

6. Start the chain again. Have the class continue the chain, adding 10–12 items. Encourage students to help one another remember the items.

Follow-up

7. Write the entire list of chained vocabulary items on the board.

Variations

To make this activity different, have students insert their own information into the drill. Ask a question that students can answer with their own information, such as "What are you going to buy at the market?" Students then chain their answers as follows: Student 1, "I'm going to buy an apple." Student 2, "She's going to buy an apple, and I'm going to buy a banana."

To make this activity more challenging, have students do this drill in small groups and see how many times they can go around the group. At the end of the activity, have each group record the items they put into the chain.

Grandma Jones Activity Suggestions

For:	Use vocabulary from:	Begin the chain drill with:
Getting Together	People and Relationships, and The Family, Dictionary, pp. 2–3	Grandma's mother is Marta, her brother is Bob, . . .
Shopping for and Preparing Food	Fruits, Dictionary, pp. 8–9	In Grandma's fruitbowl there are some apples, some bananas, . . .
Serving Food and Dining Out	Common Prepared Foods, Dictionary, p. 18	Grandma wants some fried chicken, a salad, some . . .
Buying and Describing Clothes	Everyday Clothes, Dictionary, pp. 20–21	Grandma has a yellow skirt, a black shirt, and a blue . . .
Describing Your Home	The Living Room, Dictionary, p. 28	Grandma's going to buy a sofa, a lamp, a . . .
Working Around the Home	The Utility Room, Dictionary, p. 35	Grandma has an iron, a flashlight, some lightbulbs, a . . .
Taking Care of Your Health	Ailments and Injuries, Dictionary, p. 40	Grandma has an earache, a backache, a headache, a . . .
Living in the City	The City, Dictionary, pp. 44–45	Grandma's going to the bank, the bakery, the . . .
Getting Places	The United States of America, Dictionary, pp. 72–73	Grandma's driving to Texas, Florida, California, and . . .
Talking About Jobs	Construction, Dictionary, p. 82	Grandma sees a construction worker, a builder, a . . .
Enjoying Free Time	At the Beach, Dictionary, pp. 90–91	Grandma's taking her sunglasses, a kite, a . . .

Word Toss

Focus: Listing vocabulary items.

Materials: One sheet of lined paper and one pencil per group.

Before class, select a topic from the Dictionary pages. Draw eight lines on the board. Above the lines, write a topic that is related to the selected topic. For example, if your topic is "fruit," you could write "vegetables."

Preview

1. Tell students that they will be working in small groups to make a list of words that apply to a specific topic.

Presentation

2. Invite four volunteers to the board to make a sample list. Have students number off 1–4, and take turns writing words under the topic, passing the chalk to the next student after each one has written one word. If one student gets stuck, encourage the others to suggest a word, but insist that each student write her own word. Continue for two rounds.
3. Divide the class into groups of four and have group members number off 1–4. Distribute the notebook paper and pencils to each group. Ask the 1s to write their names and pass the paper and pencil to the 2s in their group. Continue this procedure until students 1–4 have written their names.

Practice

4. Tell students the day's topic and give them five minutes to brainstorm a list of related words.

Follow-up

5. When the time limit is up, have each group count the number of words on their list. Have the group with the most words write their list on the board. Other groups can add words to the board list.
6. Direct students to the appropriate dictionary pages to check spelling.

Variation

Select one volunteer from each group to be a recorder and form a new group. Have the new group brainstorm, agree on, and list 10–12 words on an assigned topic. Then have the recorders return to their original groups and ask the group members, in turn, to guess the words on the list. When a word on the list is guessed, the recorders check it off. The first group to name all the listed words writes them on the board.

Word Toss Activity Suggestions

For:	Use vocabulary from:	To brainstorm a list of:
Getting Together	People and Relationships, Dictionary, p. 2	reasons that families get together
Shopping for and Preparing Food	Vegetables, Fruits, Meat, Poultry, and Seafood, Dictionary, pp. 6–11	vegetables, fruits, or meats
Serving Food and Dining Out	Common Prepared Foods, Dictionary, p. 18	beverages, desserts, or local restaurants
Buying and Describing Clothes	Outdoor Clothes, Everyday Clothes, Dictionary, pp. 19–21	men's or women's clothes
Describing Your Home	The Bedroom, The Bathroom, Dictionary, pp. 32 and 34	items found in the bedroom or bathroom
Working Around the Home	The Utility Room, Housework and Repair Verbs, Dictionary, pp. 35 and 38	cleaning supplies or household tasks
Taking Care of Your Health	Medical and Dental Care, Treatments and Remedies, Dictionary, pp. 39 and 41	items found in a medical office or in a medicine cabinet
Living in the City	The City, Dictionary, pp. 44–45	places in the neighborhood
Getting Places	Highway Travel, Dictionary, p. 53	different kinds of transportation
Talking About Jobs	An Office, Occupations I, II, III, Dictionary, pp. 83–86	different indoor occupations
Enjoying Free Time	Outdoor Activities, Dictionary, pp. 88–89	things you take camping

Around and Around

Focus: Asking and answering questions.

Materials: Any of the Picture Cards, pp. 180–186; or selected cue cards from the Pick a Pair activity sheet, p. 174.

Before class, select, duplicate, and cut apart a class set of picture cards or cue cards. Decide on two questions for your students to practice, and write these questions on the board; for example, using the Occupation Picture Cards, write "What does she do?"; and "Where does she work?"

Preview

1. Tell students that, using the picture cards, they will be asking and answering questions of one another, as they move around in two circles.
2. Ask students to number off 1 or 2, and to remember their numbers. Have all the 1s raise their hands, and then the 2s do likewise.
3. Invite five number 1 students to the front of the room to form an inside circle, with each student facing out. Invite four number 2 students to form an outside circle, each student facing a number 1 student. (You will face the fifth number 2 student.)
4. Model an easy question, such as "What country are you from?" for the number 1 student facing you to answer.
5. Tell only the 2s (the outside circle) to rotate two people to the right. Have all students ask and answer the model question of their new partners. Continue the procedure, varying the spaces (two students, three students) until students have returned to their original partners.
6. Explain to students your signal to stop talking and listen for directions (ringing a bell, flicking the lights on and off). Tell students that they will have about 30 seconds to exchange information.

Presentation

7. Distribute a picture or cue card to each student. Have all the 1s form an inside circle and all the 2s form an outside circle. Check that everyone has a partner. If you have an uneven number of students, have the extra person give the quiet signal on your command. Rotate this student during the activity.

Practice

8. Model the first question students will be asking about their pictures or cue cards. Have the students begin asking and answering the question until you call out the rotation directions. Walk around the circles, monitoring practice. After several rotations, introduce a new question and have the students in the outside circle exchange pictures or cards with their counterparts.

Follow-up

9. Divide students into groups of four and have them brainstorm different questions they could ask about their pictures or cards.

Around and Around Activity Suggestions

For:	Have students use:	Have students ask:
Getting Together	Students' family photos	Who is doing that? What's she doing?
Shopping for and Preparing Food	Food Picture Cards, #1–#20, p. 180	What are you buying at the market?
Serving Food and Dining Out	Prepared Food Pictures, p. 42	What would you like?
Buying and Describing Clothes	Clothing Picture Cards, #21–#40, p. 181	What size do you need? What color do you want?
Describing Your Home	Location Picture Cards, #81–#100, p. 184	Where are you? What are you doing?
Working Around the Home	Home and Tools Picture Cards, #41–#60, p. 182	What are you going to do today?
Taking Care of Your Health	Health Picture Cards, #61–#80, p. 183	What's the matter? What do you need?
Living in the City	Location Picture Cards, #81, #87–#100, p. 184	Where are you going?
Getting Places	Word cards with different states	Where are you going? How are you getting there?
Talking About Jobs	Occupation Picture Cards, #101–#120, p. 185	What does s/he do?
Enjoying Free Time	Word cards with different sports	What did you do last week? What did you play yesterday?

Instant Recall

Focus: Asking and answering questions, and testing memory.

Materials: Dictionary, selected pages; a class set of 8-1/2" x 11" scratch paper; four large sheets of lined newsprint; two markers.

Before class, select a two-page spread from the dictionary, (preferably one that includes people involved in various activities). Number 1–10 on two of the large sheets of newsprint. Label the other two sheets A and B, respectively, and post them on opposite sides of the board.

Preview

1. Tell students that they will work in two teams to ask and answer questions about a dictionary scene.
2. Direct students to study the front cover of their dictionaries for about one minute. Then have them turn the books face down. Elicit answers to the following questions: "How many people are at the bus stop?"; "What color is the girl's jacket?"; and "Is the woman looking at a newspaper?" Model the correct responses to the questions and then have volunteers look at the dictionary cover and ask you questions. Answer the students' questions and be sure to respond with "I don't know" once or twice.

Presentation

3. Model the activity by using both the front and back covers of the dictionary. Divide the class into two teams, A and B. Have each Team A student write one question about the front cover scene, and each Team B student write one question about the back cover scene. Allow time for students to write their questions.
4. Distribute the 8-1/2" x 11" scratch paper. Have each team study the opposing team's scene without writing anything down. Encourage students to try to remember as many details as possible. Give students a 3-minute time limit. When the time is up, have students quickly cover the scene with the scratch paper.
5. Invite a Team A student to read her question. Have Team B choose one student to answer the question, and encourage the other students on Team B to help their teammate. Have the A and B Teams take turns asking and answering as many questions as necessary.

Practice

6. Distribute a sheet of newsprint numbered 1–10 and a marker to each team. Explain that each team, working cooperatively, will generate ten different questions to "stump" the opposing team. Have teams choose a recorder to write down the team's questions on the newsprint.
7. Write the dictionary page for each team on the board (for example, Team A—The City, p. 44, Team B—The City, p. 45). Direct students to look at their team's page and to mask the opposite page.
8. Allow 20 minutes for the teams to generate their ten questions. Circulate and monitor student practice. After 20 minutes, collect both sheets of newsprint and post them on opposite sides of the board, covering them with the blank A and B sheets.
9. Have students study the opposing team's picture for three minutes. When the time is up, have students close their books.
10. Have one member from each team take the role of "emcee." Each emcee takes turns revealing one of her team's questions to the opposing team.

Follow-up

11. Award points for correct answers and total the points for each team. Discuss any structures or vocabulary that caused problems during the game.

Variation

Teams can use separate, but related pages, such as The Bedroom and The Bathroom, or An Office and A Classroom.

Instant Recall Activity Suggestions

For:	Team A looks at:	Team B looks at:
Getting Together	People and Relationships, Dictionary, p. 2	Seasonal Verbs, Dictionary, p. 26
Shopping for and Preparing Food	The Supermarket, Dictionary, p. 14	The Supermarket, Dictionary, p. 15
Serving Food and Dining Out	Family Restaurant and Cocktail Lounge, Dictionary, p. 16	Restaurant Verbs, Dictionary, p. 17
Buying and Describing Clothes	Outdoor Clothes, Dictionary, p. 19	Jewelry and Cosmetics, Dictionary, p. 23
Describing Your Home	The Living Room, Dictionary, p. 28	The Baby's Room, Dictionary, p. 33
Working Around the Home	Houses, Dictionary, p. 27	The Utility Room, Dictionary, p. 35
Taking Care of Your Health	Medical and Dental Care, Dictionary, p. 39	Firefighting and Rescue, Dictionary, p. 42
Living in the City	The Public Library, Dictionary, p. 47	A Classroom, Dictionary, p. 76
Getting Places	Public Transportation Dictionary, p. 55	Air Travel, Dictionary, p. 56
Talking About Jobs	Occupations II, Dictionary, p. 85	Occupations III, Dictionary, p. 86
Enjoying Free Time	Outdoor Activities, Dictionary, pp. 88–89	At the Beach, Dictionary, pp. 90–91

What's Going On Here?

Focus: Asking and answering questions.

Materials: Activity Sheet, p. 173; Don't Look Mask, p. 179; **Dictionary, selected pages.**

Before class, duplicate a class set of the activity sheet and the Don't Look Mask. Decide which pages in the dictionary you will use (the scenes with people are the most appropriate).

Preview

1. Tell students that they will be practicing giving and receiving information in small groups.
2. Direct students to the appropriate pages in their dictionaries and preview the vocabulary. Have students mask the bottom of the page and point to the pictures as you say the word.

Presentation

3. Explain any new vocabulary on the activity sheet. Give several "point to" commands, such as "Point to something at the top of the page," "Point to something small," and "Point to something you use every day."
4. Ask a student volunteer the first question on the activity sheet. Instruct her not to tell the rest of the class the answer, only the person sitting next to her. Check for comprehension by asking the person told for the answer. Repeat this comprehension check with the first question from each section on the activity sheet.

Practice

5. Divide the class into groups of three or four students and assign group leaders.
6. Distribute the activity sheets, one copy per group. Review the directions and answer any questions. Explain that the leader will divide the questions among the group members and that <u>each student in the group is</u>

<u>responsible for learning the answers given by the other members in the group.</u> Allow 5–10 minutes for students to work alone. Then have the group leader call on students to share their answers. (Some questions may have no answers.)
7. Give students a 15–20 minute time limit and walk around the room to monitor their work.

Follow-up

8. Discuss with the class which questions were the easiest to answer and which were the most difficult. Make a list on the board of the questions for which there were no answers.

Variations

To make this activity easier, divide students into groups of four or five and give each group one copy of the questions and a pair of scissors. Ask one student to cut the questions apart and to put them into a pile, face down. Have students take turns removing one question from the pile and answering it. If a student is unable to answer, she may choose another question or ask for help.

For multi-level classes, divide students into pairs and assign one partner the role of "teacher" and the other the role of "student." Have the teachers ask the questions and the students answer them. (Give the <u>less able</u> students the role of teacher.) After 5–10 minutes (more with able students), have students change roles. Explain that <u>both partners are responsible for learning all the answers.</u>

What's Going on Here? Activity Suggestions

For:	Have students use:	Or:
Getting Together	People and Relationships, Dictionary, p. 2	
Shopping for and Preparing Food	The Supermarket, Dictionary, p. 14	The Supermarket, Dictionary, p. 15
Serving Food and Dining Out	Family Restaurant and Cocktail Lounge, Dictionary, p. 16	
Buying and Describing Clothes	Everyday Clothes, Dictionary, pp. 20–21	Jewelry and Cosmetics, Dictionary, p. 23
Describing Your Home	The Baby's Room, Dictionary, p. 33	The Living Room, Dictionary, p. 28
Working Around the Home	Seasonal Verbs, Dictionary, p. 26	The Utility Room, Dictionary, p. 35
Taking Care of Your Health	Firefighting and Rescue, Dictionary, p. 42	Medical and Dental Care, Dictionary, p. 39
Living in the City	The City, Dictionary, pp. 44–45	A Classroom, Dictionary, p. 76
Getting Places	Public Transportation, Dictionary, pp. 54–55	Air Travel, Dictionary, p. 56
Talking About Jobs	Farming and Ranching, Dictionary, p. 81	Occupations III, Dictionary, p. 86
Enjoying Free Time	Neighborhood Parks, Dictionary, pp. 87	At the Beach, Dictionary, pp. 90–91

Pick a Pair

> **Focus:** Identifying and matching vocabulary items.
>
> **Materials:** Activity sheet, p. 174; selected Picture Cards, pp. 180–186; six 8-1/2″ x 11″ sheets of paper; paper clips.
>
> ---
>
> *Before class, duplicate one copy of the activity sheet. Select and duplicate eight picture cards. Paste these pictures, at random, on the activity sheet. Write the corresponding vocabulary on the remaining eight squares. Duplicate and cut apart half a class set of this picture/word page. Separate the picture/word cards into sets and clip them together. On the six 8-1/2″ x 11″ sheets of paper, draw three of the selected picture cards, and write the three matching vocabulary words.*

Preview

1. Tell students that they will be working in pairs to match pictures and words.
2. Mix up the 8-1/2″ x 11″ cards and place them on the chalk ledge, face down. Invite a volunteer to pick two cards and show them to the class. Have students identify both the picture and word card, then ask "Do they match?" Repeat the procedure until all six cards have been revealed.

Presentation

3. Pair students and give each pair a picture/word card set. Have partners place their cards face down on their desks.
4. Tell students that they will take turns picking two cards from their set and identifying a "match" or "no match." Explain that students must call out the names for both the picture and word cards, and that the activity ends when all the cards are matched.

5. Have one pair demonstrate the activity, with one partner picking two picture/word cards while the other calls out "match" or "no match."

Practice

6. Set a 15-minute time limit and have students begin the activity. When pairs finish, have them re-shuffle their cards and play again.

Follow-up

7. Have partners turn their cards face up and listen to your definition or description of the vocabulary items. As you define the word, each partner holds up the appropriate card, (one partner takes the word card, the other takes the picture card). Invite stronger students to give definitions or descriptions to the rest of the class.

Variations

To make this activity easier, have students match pictures only. Select and duplicate two copies of the eight pictures from the Picture Card page and paste the pictures, at random, on the activity sheet.

To make this activity more challenging, have advanced students create a sentence using the vocabulary from each match, such as (apple) "I have an apple in my refrigerator." or "Apple pie is delicious for dessert."

Pick a Pair Activity Suggestions

For:	Use pictures and/or vocabulary from:	To create cards with:
Getting Together	The Family, Dictionary, p. 3	Matching male/female relatives (aunt/uncle) from The Family, p. 3
Shopping for and Preparing Food	Food Picture Cards, #1–#20, p. 180	Grocery items and matching vocabulary
Serving Food and Dining Out	Prepared Food Pictures, p. 42	Prepared food items and matching vocabulary
Buying and Describing Clothes	Clothing Picture Cards, #21–#40, p. 181	Clothing items and matching vocabulary
Describing Your Home	Home and Tool Picture Cards #41–#50, p. 182	Furniture and matching vocabulary
Working Around the Home	Home and Tool Picture Cards #51–#60, p. 182	Household tools and matching vocabulary
Taking Care of Your Health	Health Picture Cards, #61–#80, p. 183	Ailments or Treatments and matching vocabulary
Living in the City	Location Picture Cards, #81, #87–#100, p. 184	Places in the city and matching vocabulary
Getting Places	Highway Travel, and Public Transportation, Dictionary, pp. 53–55	Vehicles and matching occupations (bus, bus driver)
Talking About Jobs	Occupation Picture Cards, #101–#120, p. 185	Occupations and matching vocabulary
Enjoying Free Time	Individual Sports, Dictionary, p. 94	Sports and matching equipment (tennis/tennis racket)

Twin Grids

Focus: Listening for and giving instructions.

Materials: Activity sheet, p. 175; selected Picture Cards, pp. 180–186; two 8-1/2″ x 11″ blank sheets of paper; manila folders (one per pair); paper clips.

Before class, choose a topic from the Dictionary or use the Twin Grid activity suggestions on page 169. Duplicate a class set of the activity sheet. Duplicate and cut apart a class set of the appropriate picture cards. (Or use the vocabulary from a dictionary page to fill in the squares on the Pick a Pair activity sheet, p. 174. Duplicate and cut apart a class set of this sheet.) Clip each picture or word card set to an activity sheet. Copy two of the pictures (or words) onto the 8-1/2″ x 11″ sheets of paper.

Preview

1. Tell students that they will be working in pairs to arrange pictures (or words) according to their partner's instructions.

2. Draw a large blank grid on the board similar to that on the activity sheet. Call out the numbers 1–16 at random, as different students come up to the board and point to the correct square.

3. Place the 8-1/2″ x 11″ pictures face up on the chalk ledge. Invite a volunteer to the front of the room and model the command: "Find the (apple) _____. Put it in _____ (#1)." Get class consensus on the correct picture and its placement on the grid. Repeat the procedure with another volunteer.

Presentation

4. Distribute an activity sheet and a set of picture or word cards to each student. Have students place their cards face up on their desks. Model the activity by instructing students where to place their cards on their

grids. Check accuracy by pointing to the correct square on the board as students check their own grids.

5. Pair students and assign each an A or a B role. Distribute a manila folder to each pair, to be propped up between the students as a screen. Tell students they will take turns telling their partner where to place the 16 cards on the grids. Explain that while they are directing their partners, they are simultaneously placing the identical cards on their own grids. Instruct students to look only at their own grids and not at their partner's.

6. Have one volunteer pair demonstrate the activity for the class, placing only four to five of the cards.

Practice

7. Set a time limit of 15 minutes and have the A students begin directing the B students. When pairs have finished, have them remove the manila folder and check to see if they have identical or "twin" grids. Then tell the B students to direct the A students. Circulate and monitor student practice.

Follow-up

8. Have different students direct you as you complete the grid on the board. Write the vocabulary items or draw the pictures in the appropriate squares.

Variations

To make this activity easier, put a transparency of the grid on an overhead projector and do the activity with the whole class. Duplicate and cut apart a transparency of selected picture or word cards. Have volunteers come up and place the pictures according to your directions or invite students to direct their classmates.

To make this activity more challenging, have stronger students describe, rather than name, each picture to their partner: "You wear this when it's very cold. Put it on #2." *(jacket)*

Twin Grids Activity Suggestions

For:	Use pictures and/or vocabulary from:	To create cards with:
Getting Together	The Family, Dictionary, p. 3	Family vocabulary
Shopping for and Preparing Food	Food Picture Cards, #1–#20, p. 180	Grocery items
Serving Food and Dining Out	Prepared Food Pictures, p. 42	Prepared food items
Buying and Describing Clothes	Clothing Picture Cards, #21–#40, p. 181	Clothing items
Describing Your Home	Home and Tools Picture Cards, #41–#52, p. 182 and Location Picture Cards, #81–#85, p. 185	Furniture and rooms in the house
Working Around the House	A Workshop, Dictionary, pp. 36–37	Workshop tools
Taking Care of Your Health	Health Picture Cards, #61–#80, p. 183	Ailments or Treatments
Living in the City	The U.S. Postal System, Dictionary, p. 46	Post office vocabulary
Getting Places	Cars, Dictionary, pp. 50–51	Parts of the car
Talking About Jobs	Occupation Picture Cards, #101–#120, p. 185	Occupations
Enjoying Free Time	Team Sports, and Individual Sports, Dictionary, pp. 92 and 94	Sports

Back and Forth Bingo

> *Focus:* Asking and answering yes/no questions.
>
> *Materials:* Activity sheet, p. 176; selected Picture Cards, pp. 180–186.
>
> ---
>
> *Before class, choose a dictionary topic for the activity, and decide upon a yes/no structure to be practiced, such as "Are you . . . ?"; "Do you . . . ?"; "Can you . . . ?"; "Did you . . . ?"; "Were you . . . ?"; "Are you going to . . . ?"; or "Will you . . . ?" Duplicate one copy of the activity sheet. Choose, duplicate, and cut apart 16 appropriate pictures from the picture card pages to serve as cues for the yes/no questions. Paste the pictures on the squares on the activity sheet grid. Write the sample yes/no question at the top of the sheet and on the board. Duplicate a class set of the activity sheet.*

Preview

1. Tell students that they will be walking around the classroom asking each other yes/no questions about the topic of the day. Explain that students will be trying to get yes answers and four different signatures in a row on their activity sheets to get BINGO!
2. Direct students to look at the appropriate page(s) in their dictionaries. Model the sample yes/no question on the board, using vocabulary on the page(s). Have the class practice the question, substituting other vocabulary on the page.

Presentation

3. Distribute the activity sheet and ask students to practice the yes/no question using the first four pictures. Then have students put their sheets down and watch as you ask different questions of individual students. When a student answers yes to a question, have the student sign your paper in the appropriate square. When a student answers no to a question, explain that the student

may not sign the square. Emphasize that each student can sign your paper one time only. When you have four different signatures in a row, call out "BINGO!" Show students the diagonal, horizontal, and vertical rows that lead to BINGO on the board. If necessary, have several volunteers demonstrate the activity in front of the class.

Practice

4. Tell students that they will have 10 minutes to play the game. Ask students to call out BINGO! and check with you as soon as they get four signatures in a row. Have students pick up their activity sheets, stand up, and start asking questions.
5. As students get BINGO and come to you, number their activity sheets, in order, and send the students back into the activity to continue asking questions until time is up.

Follow-up

6. Check the accuracy of the answers on activity sheets numbered 1–5 (the first five students' papers) by asking questions, such as "Paul, do you like carrots?" Use the names of the students whose signatures appear on the various activity sheet squares.

Variations

To make this activity easier, use 9 squares rather than 16. Delete the outer squares on the activity sheet.

To make this activity more challenging, instruct students to get as many yes answers as possible from the class, in order to fill their BINGO grid. Students can have a person sign their paper more than once. Suggest that students can help direct one another to people with yes answers: "No, I don't fix cars, but Juan does."

Back and Forth BINGO Activity Suggestions

For:	Fill in the BINGO sheet with:	Have students ask:
Getting Together	Vocabulary from The Family, Dictionary, p. 3	Are you living with your . . . ?
Shopping for and Preparing Food	Food Picture Cards, #1–#20, p. 180	Did you ever eat . . . ?
Serving Food and Dining Out	Prepared Food Pictures, p. 42	Do you like . . . ?
Buying and Describing Clothes	Clothing Picture Cards, #21–#40, p. 181	Do you have a . . . in your closet?
Describing Your Home	Furniture vocabulary from The Living Room, The Bedroom, The Baby's Room, Dictionary, pp. 28, 32–33	Is there a . . . in your home?
Working Around the House	Vocabulary from The Utility Room, Dictionary, p. 35	Do you have a . . . ?
Taking Care of Your Health	Health Picture Cards #61–#80, p. 183	Did you ever . . . ?
Living in the City	Location Picture Cards, #87–#100, p. 184	Are you going to . . . this weekend?
Getting Places	Names of 16 states from The United States, Dictionary, pp. 72–73	Can you spell . . . ?
Talking About Jobs	Occupation Picture Cards, #101–#120, p. 185	Can you . . . ?
Enjoying Free Time	Vocabulary from At the Beach, Dictionary, pp. 90–91	Where do you buy a . . . ?

Your Notes

What's Going on Here? (See Teacher's Notes, page 164.)

- Divide into small groups. Choose a leader.
- Divide the questions among the students in your group.
- Each student finds the answers to his or her own questions.
- The leader asks everyone to share his or her answers.

Descriptions

1. What is at the top of the page?

2. What is in the middle of the page?

3. What is at the bottom of the page?

4. What is small?

5. What is large?

6. Is this picture inside or outside?

People and Actions

7. How many people do you see?

8. What are people talking about?

9. What are people doing?

10. What occupations do you see?

11. Where are people going?

12. What is a person holding in his or her hands?

13. What are people looking at?

Using and Buying Things

14. What is used every day?

15. What is used once a week?

16. What costs a lot of money?

17. What costs a little money?

18. What is something you cannot buy?

Pick a Pair (See Teacher's Notes, page 166.)

■ Cut apart the picture and word cards.
■ Mix up the cards and turn them over in front of you.
■ Take turns choosing two cards and turning them over.
■ When the cards match, take them.
■ When they don't match, put them back.

Pick a Pair

Twin Grids (See Teacher's Notes, page 168.)

- Don't look at your partner's grid.
- Student 1: Put a picture on your grid, tell your partner where it is.
- Student 2: Listen and put the picture on your grid.
- When you have a picture on each square, compare grids.

1	2	3	4
5	6	7	8
9	10	11	12
13	14	15	16

Back and Forth Bingo (See Teacher's Notes, page 170.)

■ Ask your classmates the question.
■ When your classmates answer "yes," they can sign the squares.
■ When your classmates answer "no," they can't sign the squares.
■ Get different signatures for each square.
■ When you get four signatures in a row, you have BINGO!

Ask your classmates			

Answer Card/Don't Look Mask Picture Cards #1–#140

Food	**#1–#20**
Clothing	**#21–#40**
Home and Tools	**#41–#60**
Health	**#61–#80**
Locations	**#81–#100**
Occupations	**#101–#120**
Actions	**#121–#140**

NOT SURE

NO

YES

DON'T LOOK

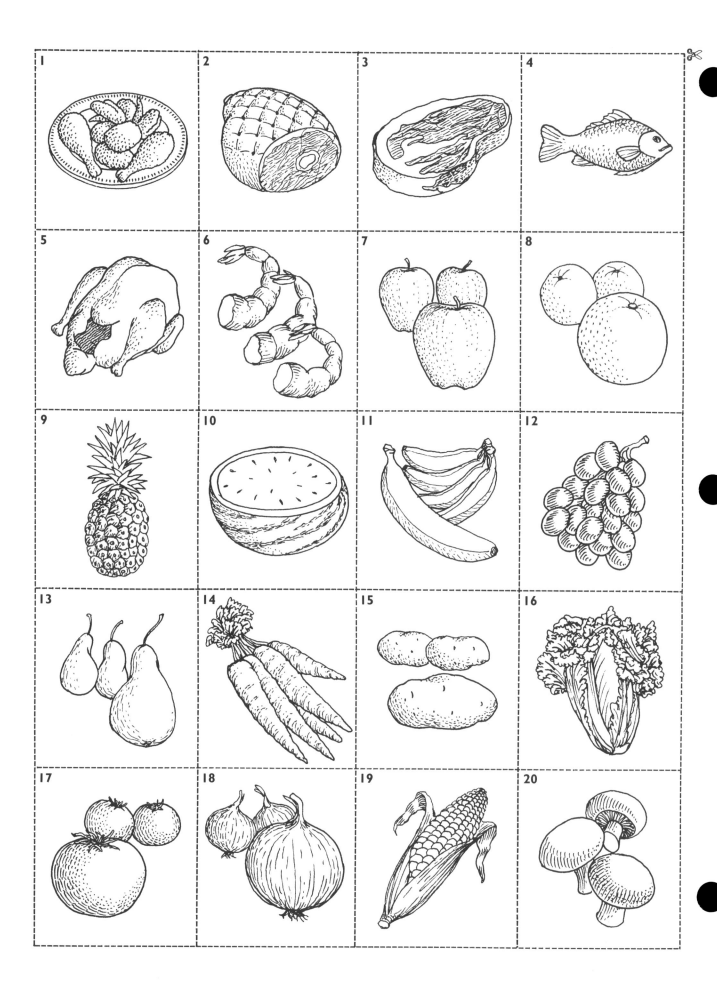

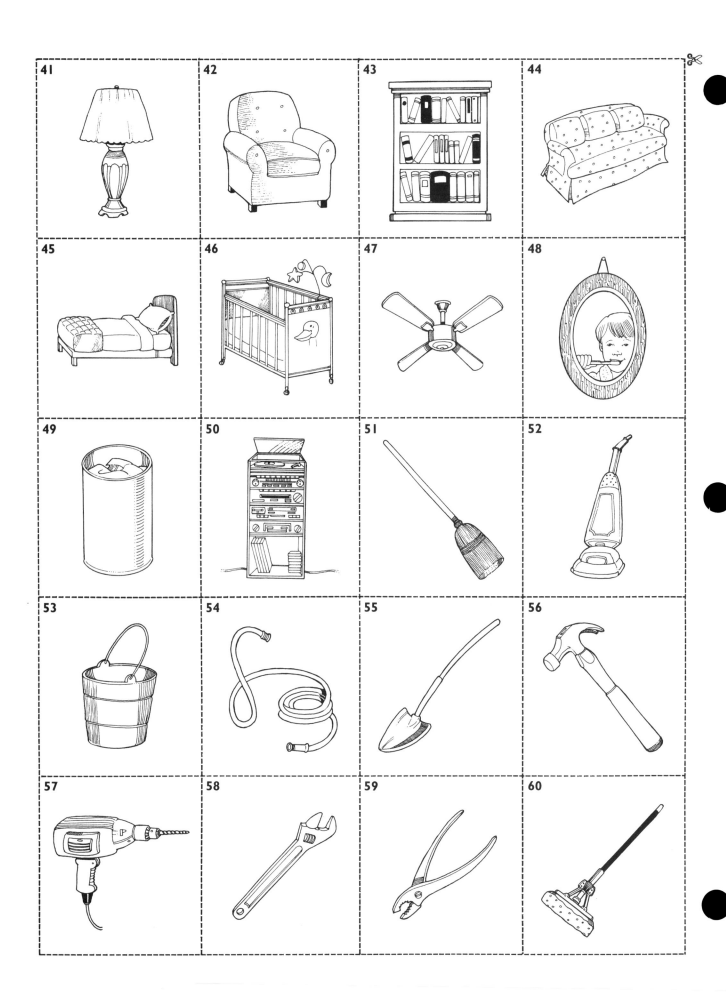

Index